Twayne's English Authors Series

EDITOR OF THIS VOLUME

Herbert Sussman

NORTHEASTERN UNIVERSITY

*The Nineteenth-Century
Anglo-Jewish Novel*

TEAS 295

THE NINETEENTH-CENTURY ANGLO-JEWISH NOVEL

By LINDA GERTNER ZATLIN

Morehouse College

TWAYNE PUBLISHERS
A DIVISION OF G.K. HALL & CO. BOSTON

Published 1981 by Twayne Publishers,
A Division of G. K. Hall & Co.
All Rights Reserved

Printed on permanent/durable acid-free paper and bound
in the United States of America

First Printing

Frontispiece photo courtesy of Dr. Alan Lease

Library of Congress Cataloging in Publication Data

Zatlin, Linda Gertner.
The nineteenth—century anglo-Jewish novel.

(Twayne's English authors series ; TEAS 295)
Bibliography: p. 146-52
Includes index.
1.   English fiction—Jewish authors—History and criticism.
2.   English fiction—19th century—History and criticism.
3.   Jews in literature.
I.   Title.
PR868.J4Z37   823'.009'8924   80-25147
ISBN 0-8057-6787-8

For
my parents,
Jonathan, and Andrew

Contents

About the Author

Linda Gertner Zatlin is an Associate Professor of English at Morehouse College. She has been a member of the faculty there since 1967.

She has contributed articles on drama, poetry, and fiction to *Obsidian,* the *University of Michigan Papers in Women's Studies, Critique, Éthique et ésthétique dans la littérature Française du XX siècle,* and the *Victorian Newsletter.* Her major research interest is the way in which social attitudes, particularly toward minorities, are transmitted by the novel. She is currently working on establishing the relationship between characters and their religious views in nineteenth-century Anglo-Jewish novels and in George Eliot's *Daniel Deronda.*

She is cofounder and currently Secretary-Treasurer of the *Southeastern Nineteenth-Century Studies Association.*

Preface

Although much has been written about figures such as Rebecca and Isaac of York, Fagin, Riah, Daniel Deronda, and Svengali, it is sometimes forgotten that nineteenth-century fictional explorations of the Jew were also undertaken by Anglo-Jewish novelists. From the 1840s to the turn of the century, thirty-two novels by fifteen Anglo-Jewish writers record varying responses to the external and internal pressures faced by Victorian Jews. Addressed to a dual audience of Christians and Jews, most of these novels display a keen interest in the fictional delineation of the pleasures and pains of being a Jew in the nineteenth century.

This study of the thirty-two known novels by Anglo-Jewish novelists provides an introduction to the history of the Jew in England and to the novels by Anglo-Jews together with a social window on works of a minority group historically disdained, financially feared, and literarily detested, yet who influenced British history, economics, and literature. It offers as well a glimpse of the precedents for some twentieth-century stereotypes in fiction—the Jewish mother, the Jewish princess, the meek Jewish husband, and the alienated Jew—and an idea of why and how these stereotypes arose.

However popular these novels may have been at the time, today few are read. With the exception of the works of Israel Zangwill, they present little of the moral vision, prophecy, or for that matter characterization which marks a work of fiction as art. Insofar as literature echoes social phenomena, they do, however, provide fascinating insight into the nineteenth-century Jew's position within both the English and the Anglo-Jewish community. These novels were written largely in response to negative English views of Jews and to portions of the Anglo-Jewish community.

That a response to Victorian attitudes toward Jews was called for during the nineteenth century was expressed by Zangwill, who, in a political context, explains, "If there were no Jews, they would have to be invented, for the use of politicians—they are indispensable, the antithesis of a panacea; guaranteed to *cause* all evils."[1] Zangwill cannot be accused of special pleading, for, in the minds of many Englishmen and women from the early thirteenth century forward, the position of blame was occupied by Jews.

The term, "Jew," used roughly for six centuries by most non-Jewish dramatists, poets, and novelists, evoked particular historical, religious, literary, and mythical undertones as well as atavistic fear. As an allusion, the word "Jew" for some connoted rootlessness, unmitigated evil, social disintegration, rapacity, and unregenerate humanity, to mention a few well-known concepts. These concepts constituted a familiar negative stereotype inherited by nineteenth-century novelists. Whether an author used the appellation consciously or unconsciously, the result was often the same. For example, whether Dickens was anti-Semitic or not, when he calls Fagin (*Oliver Twist*, 1838) "the Jew," he draws on religious bias as well as the historical and literary anti-Semitic tradition. Fagin is not simply an unregenerate man, he is an unregenerate Jew. By no means is *every* portrait of a Jew who is evil or criminal or even imperfect an anti-Semitic portrayal. Fagin is evil in a stereotypical manner that specifically plays on traditional anti-Semitism. Had he been Jewish and evil or sinister like Dickens's Murdstone, Tulkinghorn, Compeyson, or Bradley Headstone, the stereotypical associations, fundamentally anti-Semitic, would not be aroused. With Fagin, however, biblical and other religious references trigger associations of his character and his evil with his religion.

Moreover, whatever moral views authors are presumed to possess, they fall prey to popular prejudiced notions no less than the audience that sympathetically reads their work. A Jew could not be accurately portrayed by Chaucer or Marlowe, perhaps because their frames of reference did not include real Jews (although Shakespeare succeeds far more under the same conditions), but neither would their respective audiences have accepted a balanced, realistic Jewish character. Nineteenth-century novelists, writing at a time when negative attitudes toward Jews continued to be voiced, should not be assumed to be wholly different. Fagin is merely the most celebrated early nineteenth-century example.

The response to the English provides but one reason Anglo-Jewish novels were written. Their authors also saw problems within their own community which they wanted to correct. In emigrating from Eastern Europe, Jews had to learn to live outside of locked ghettoes. In *Children of the Ghetto* (1892) Zangwill says of the European immigrant, "He yearned to approximate as much as possible to John Bull without merging in him; to sink himself and yet not be absorbed, not to be and yet to be. . . . For such is the nature of Jeshurun. [The poetic name for Israel and thus the Jews, Jeshurun means righteous, upright, and beloved.] Enfranchise him, give him his own way and you make a new man of him; persecute him and he is himself again";[2] Zangwill's purview is historical fact. In most European ghettoes contact with the outside world was minimal—by Christian law. Frankfort Jews were not allowed outside, even to bury their dead. In England the situation was very different. Although Jews were under political restrictions, these were in no manner like locked ghetto gates. Within this more liberal setting Jews had to define new rules and chart new ways. Should they fully accommodate to English society and forget about Judaism? Should they remain separate from people not of their religion? Fully? Partially? Should they try to find a balance? These questions, even as they must have been asked and answered by Anglo-Jews, were asked and answered by Anglo-Jewish novelists.

In order to obtain the sharpest definition of the Anglo-Jewish novel and of Anglo-Jewish attitudes, I have organized this study around three challenges responded to by Anglo-Jewish novelists— anti-Semitism, appeals to convert, and problems within the Anglo-Jewish community. I have omitted writers like Helene Gingold and Israel Cohen, who published only short stories, as well as novels which do not *detail* but merely refer incidentally to Jewish life (for example, Joseph Jacobs, *As Others Saw Him; A Retrospect A.D. 54*, 1903, and Samuel Gordon's *The Lost Kingdom; or, the Passing of the Khazars*, 1926). In addition, I have excluded the most famous nineteenth-century apostate, Benjamin Disraeli, as well as other novelists of Jewish birth who embraced Christianity, and have chosen to focus instead on novels written by Jews born of a Jewish mother who did not formally renounce their religion (for a complete list of these novelists and their work, see the Bibliography). I have included discussions of novels published after the turn of the century by Anglo-Jewish novelists who began publishing prior to 1900.

Biographical information on most of these novelists is almost nonexistent. In addition to sources at the British Museum, I have consulted at the Mocatta library of Anglo-Judaica, University College, University of London; the *Transactions of the Jewish Historical Society of England;* and the *Jewish Chronicle*, the oldest, continuously published Anglo-Jewish newspaper, which is unfortunately not indexed. Olga Samech and Beth-Zion Abrahams, Anglo-Jewish writers, provided me with some additional information and much commiseration. What I discovered about each novelist appears before the discussion of his or her work.

Chapter 1 provides an introduction to the history of the Jews in England in the light of the three challenges met by Anglo-Jewish novelists. Subsequent chapters analyze the novelists' responses. Chapters 2, 3, and 4 deal with their answers to the challenges of anti-Semitism and conversion: the plea for English tolerance, the plea to Jews to remain Orthodox (I capitalize the term throughout to remind the reader of the distinction between the two branches into which Judaism split during the nineteenth century: Orthodox and Reform), and the Jewish counter to the English stereotype of the Jew. Chapters 5 and 6 survey the novelists' replies to the challenge of the Anglo-Jewish community. Chapter 6 also considers the works of Israel Zangwill, the best and most widely known of these novelists, in relation to the three challenges and suggests why Zangwill continues to attract a readership. Chapter 7 examines the wider impact of Anglo-Jewish fiction.

A number of people have assisted me in this study, and I would like to thank them. Professors Jerome Beaty, J. Paul Hunter, and Ronald Schuchard of Emory University read early drafts. Professors Uli Knoepflmacher of Princeton and Sara Putzell of the Georgia Institute of Technology were particularly helpful with organization and later drafts. My typist, Josephine Zachery, typed pleasantly despite my pressure. I would also like to acknowledge Dr. Alan Lease for his superb photography. To my sons, Jonathan and Andrew, I owe the largest debt of gratitude for their assistance in proofreading and in searching out biblical passages as well as for their intelligence in discussing ideas with me, and most of all for their encouragement and unfailing love.

LINDA GERTNER ZATLIN

Morehouse College
Atlanta, Georgia

Chronology

Included are selected dates in Anglo-Jewish history and first publication dates of short stories and novels.

1290   Expulsion from England.
1656   Readmission to England.
1722   Allowed to own land.
1809   Society for Promoting Christianity among Jews founded.
1830   Catholic Emancipation Act.
1830s   Jewish Board of Deputies founded.
1831   Trade restrictions removed.
1835   First Jewish Sheriff of London elected. *Hebrew Intelligencer* founded.
1840   Celia and Marian Moss, *The Romance of Jewish History*. The Damascus Affair.
1841   West London (Reform) Synagogue founded. *Voice of Jacob* and *Jewish Chronicle* founded.
1842   Samuel Phillips, *Caleb Stukely*.
1843   Celia and Marian Moss, *Tales of Jewish History*.
1844   Grace Aguilar, *Records of Israel*.
1845   Charlotte Montefiore, *Caleb Asher*. Jews eligible for election to London municipal offices.
1850   Grace Aguilar, *The Vale of Cedars; or, the Martyr*.
1853   Grace Aguilar, *Home Scenes and Heart Studies*.
1855   First Jewish Lord Mayor of London elected. Jews' College opened.
1857   Matthias Levy, *The Hasty Marriage; A Sketch of Modern Jewish Life*.
1858   Removal of civil and legal disabilities; Jews eligible for election to the House of Commons.
1859   Board of Guardians for Relief of the Jewish Poor founded.
1865   Celia Moss Levetus, *The King's Physician and Other Tales*.
1866   Jews eligible for election to the House of Lords.
1871   Anglo-Jewish Association founded. University Tests Act. Factory Act.

1872	Ballot Act.
1873	*Jewish World* begins publication.
1875	Benjamin Farjeon, *At the Sign of the Silver Flagon.*
1876	Benjamin Farjeon, *Solomon Isaacs; A Novel.*
1878	Emily Marian Harris, *Estelle.*
1881	Russo-Jewish Committee formed.
1887	Emily Marian Harris, *Benedictus.* Julia Frankau, *Dr. Phillips; A Maida Vale Idyll.*
1888	Amy Levy, *Reuben Sachs; A Sketch.*
1889	Amy Levy, "Cohen of Trinity." Julia Frankau, *A Babe in Bohemia.*
1890	Oswald John Simon, *The World and the Cloister.*
1892	Israel Zangwill, *Children of the Ghetto; A Study of a Peculiar People.*
1893	Israel Zangwill, *Ghetto Tragedies.*
1894	Mrs. Alfred Sidgwick, *Lesser's Daughter.* Benjamin Farjeon, *Aaron the Jew.* Israel Zangwill, *The King of Schnorrers.*
1895	Isadore G. Ascher, *The Doom of Destiny.* Mrs. Alfred Sidgwick, *Grasshoppers.*
1896	Mrs. Alfred Sidgwick, *A Woman with a Future.*
1897	Samuel Gordon, *A Handful of Exotics.* Zionist Organization founded.
1898	Samuel Gordon, *The Daughters of Shem.* Israel Zangwill, *Dreamers of the Ghetto.*
1900	Samuel Gordon, *Sons of the Covenant; A Tale of London Jewry.* Benjamin Farjeon, *Pride of Race.*
1902	Samuel Gordon, *Strangers at the Gate.*
1903	Samuel Gordon, *The Queen's Quandary.* Julia Frankau, *Pigs in Clover.*
1904	Mrs. Alfred Sidgwick, *Scenes of Jewish Life.* Samuel Gordon, *Unto Each Man His Own.*
1906	Samuel Gordon, *The Ferry of Fate.* Julia Frankau, *The Sphinx's Lawyer.*
1907	Israel Zangwill, *Ghetto Comedies.*
1916	Samuel Gordon, *God's Remnants.*
1917	Balfour Declaration.
1918	Mrs. Alfred Sidgwick, *The Devil's Cradle.*
1919	Mrs. Alfred Sidgwick, *Iron Cousins.*
1934	Mrs. Alfred Sidgwick, *Refugee.*

CHAPTER 1

Introductory: The Jews in England

B Y 1830, Jews in England were more secure, better educated, and larger in number than ever before. In that year the Catholic Emancipation Act passed, signaling increased English toleration of minorities. For the first time Anglo-Jewish novelists saw themselves as able to respond actively to three challenges which faced them. The first two were historical conditions within English society. The third challenge was created by contemporary changes inside the Jewish community. The first challenge was the pervasive anti-Semitic tradition that goes back to the expulsion of Jews from England under Edward I. The second challenge, closely related in nature, was the attempt to convert Jews, first formalized and methodically undertaken by the Society for Promoting Christianity among Jews, founded in 1809. The third challenge came from within rather than without and came later. In the latter half of the century, Jewish novelists responded to internal problems in the Anglo-Jewish community: intermarriage, assimilation, the shift away from Ortho-dox Judaism, and the influx of more immigrants. Throughout the century the novelists addressed Christians and Jews. Their novels are informed by their consciousness of the nineteenth-century Jew's position in England, a position shaped largely by anti-Semitism.

I *The First Challenge*

The first challenge originated with William the Conqueror's shrewd invitation to French Jews to settle in England to aid his economic policies. Anti-Semitism was generated almost at once. Although initially granted protection by the first three Norman kings to facilitate the royal treasury's operation, Jews immediately distinguished themselves from the general population by dress, dietary laws, worship, and occupations; they lived in Jewries by their own choice. Because of these differences, they were suspected by hostile, uncomprehending commoners who watched Jews accrete wealth they believed was rightfully theirs. Jews were despised also by aristocratic barons who owed them money. Beginning during the eleventh century, the Crusades, cries of usurer or Christ-killer, and accusations of ritual murder, supported by an already hostile populace, combined to end Jewish tranquility in England.[1]

One infamous example of the ritual murder charge occurred in 1255. Young Hugh of Lincoln was found dead. The Jews of Lincoln were accused of torturing and crucifying him in a re-creation of Jesus Christ's martyrdom, then of using his blood for ritual purposes. The charge was false, but most of the Jewish populace was murdered. From 1144 until they were finally impoverished and therefore of no further use to the Crown, Jews were persecuted by royal extortion, clerical oppression, and periodic popular massacres fanned by superstition.[2] The barons had a heavy hand in massacres and in events leading up to the Jews' expulsion from England, seeing these as easy ways both of liquidating their debts to Jewish moneylenders and of damming the king's source of money, thus checking royal control over them. Although the Jews had requested permission to leave England in 1250, it was not until 1290 that Edward I, sensitive to Rome's pleasure, expelled the total Anglo-Jewish population which, then at its early peak, numbered 16,500. The overt motives behind the expulsion were economic and political: the Jews fell victim to the constant power struggle between the Crown and the semi-autonomous nobility, becoming the scapegoat for the crises and disasters which had struck England.

Although from 1290 to 1656 Jews were officially barred from living in England, they did not completely disappear from English records or memory. In addition to a number of converts to Judaism, Jewish physicians, men of law, and financiers served Henry IV, Henry VIII, Elizabeth I, and Cromwell, residing in England under the Crown's protection. These few Jews had no organized community. Moreover, they did not make themselves generally known as Jews. Nonetheless, popular anti-Jewish sentiment sustained itself, particularly in ballads and tales memorializing Hugh of Lincoln and the Wandering Jew.

Through the early seventeenth century most of the small number of Jews in England resided in the university towns. There was also a London settlement of Sephardic Marrano[3] merchants who, because of their widespread commercial connections, were of service to the English government as diplomats. Considering Jews' successful commercial and banking activities on the Continent, Cromwell, already sympathetic toward those affected by religious persecution, was favorably disposed to Jewish readmission to England. In this benevolent environment the Sephardic community, which had been using the protective facade of Catholicism, grew. In 1656, in response to the petition for protection as Jews, Cromwell was able to grant Jews already living in England unrestricted rights of residence and trade. 1656 is commonly called the "resettlement" in Anglo-Jewish history.

As they had formerly paid for royal protection by being permitted to channel money into royal coffers, Jews now paid for rights in coin of a different tender. In return for residence and trade protection, they were required to promise not to encourage immigration, not to allow their religious ceremonies to obtrude on the public, not to engage in controversies, and not to seek converts. Nonetheless, English Jewry, consisting of thirty-five Sephardic families, had found security. It was late in coming—England was the last non-Catholic country in which no formal Jewish community was to be found— but now Jews could live undisguised and relatively untroubled. Moreover, Cromwell's canny foresight paid off. The first Jewish settlers not only brought capital of one and a half million pounds in hard cash when it was sorely needed by the government, but their annual turnover in trade equalled one-twelfth of the total trade of England. Jews quickly made their new home the center of international commerce.[4]

After 1656 Cossack uprisings drove Jews westward from Russia and swelled the English Jewish settlement until in 1800 it numbered approximately 26,000, still less than .003 percent of the total population of England and Wales.[5] The London community housed 20,000 people and remained the most important and influential one. During this period of one and a half centuries, some indigent, immigrant Jews settled in the provinces. Most Jews began work at the lowest mercantile stage—peddling. Many progressed from street traders to shopkeepers to merchants, concurrently providing tangible material from which the stage Jew as a comic, old clothes peddler was molded. When each stopped peddling and opened a store in a country town, he became the nucleus of a Jewish community. Some of these settlers became bankers.[6] Later generations established factories and mills. But the bulk of the Jewish populace was most familiarly known, it would seem from the dramas especially, as peddlers, although by 1840 the number of Jewish peddlers had sharply declined. By 1900 English Jewry had increased almost tenfold: a quarter-million Jews resided in England, representing slightly more than .0075 percent of the total population.

Despite the known wealth of a small number of mercantile families, the majority of seventeenth- and eighteenth-century London Jews were either marginally employed or totally dependent upon Jewish philanthropy. Only by 1880 could a solid fifty percent of the Jewish community be considered middle class and the poor clearly in the minority.[7] The Sephardim assumed responsibility for relief of the Sephardic indigent as they arrived in England. The Ashkenazim were not prepared to assume their burden, and at first the Sephardim totally aided the Ashkenazic poor. By 1780 Ashkenazic immigrants received a portion of their relief from the established Ashkenazic community. Relief to indigents came directly from the synagogue of each community. In addition to the settlement of immigrants, the synagogues provided money for pensions, dowers, loans, grants, food, clothing, maternity and medical needs, apprenticeships as well as for the establishment of almshouses and homes for the sick or aged.[8]

Moreover, most retail trades were closed to Jews. Even had they been open, because of their different Sabbath, Jews could work only four and a half days per week. Furthermore, they were classed as aliens. Jews consequently lacked all political and most economic rights and could thus not hold any position of trust granted by the Crown. Most of the skilled professions refused to apprentice Jews. As a result, most poor, working Jews at this time were peddlers.

During the eighteenth century, for those Jews who could not obtain jobs nor live on philanthropy, peddling remained a major source of income. Stealing and trading became two additional sources. Around 1771 gangs of Jewish thieves formed of destitute immigrants flourished, and London saw a rapid growth of self-employed street peddlers and an underground mercantile community. (The English public remained unaware of this social problem until one gang of thieves attracted notoriety about this time.)[9] Jews generally wanted their children to learn a trade so they would not be forced to peddle in the streets. Although their aim was partially realized in 1797, when Joshua Van Oven, a London surgeon, founded Jews' Hospital to care for the aged and to employ young people, it was imperative for Jews to enter trades and for more

Jewish employers to materialize. Restrictions against London Jews in certain retail trades were not removed until 1831, however, at which time the English economy could not immediately accommodate the vast majority of Jews desiring work.[10] The problem of unemployment continued thorough the nineteenth century, becoming more troublesome during 1881—1882 and 1890—1891, when the waves of Jewish refugees became almost more responsibility than the Jewish community could handle, despite the wider range of occupations open to Jews since 1853.[11]

Moreover, within their own group, sharp distinctions existed between the few wealthy and the many poor, preponderantly Ashkenazic, Jews. The primary desire of wealthy nineteenth-century Jews was to participate in the English political process. Those Jews who had prospered in England during the seventeenth and eighteenth centuries were loyal to the Crown. For example, Nathan Mayer Rothschild, head of the House of Rothschild's London branch, demonstrated his staunch loyalty during the first two decades of the nineteenth century when he wagered his personal fortune on Napoleon's eventual defeat; in 1819 alone his bank loaned two million pounds to the English government.[12]

By 1837 when Victoria was crowned, 30,000 Jews were living in England; the House of Rothschild was firmly established; and other banking families had risen in prominence. The Goldsmids, the Mocattas, the Montagues, the Montefiores, and the Solomons had achieved international eminence. During the depression of the 1840s when men lost jobs and people starved, these bankers and brokers suffered verbal abuse because of rumors that Jews ran the commercial and financial worlds. The rumors had no basis in fact, but the scions of these families would be caricatured in English novels of the 1860s and 1870s as their fathers had been satirized earlier in poems. The fact was that by the 1850s some Jewish families had amassed solid fortunes, and they devoted themselves to securing emancipation for Jews in England and the rest of Europe. England felt and responded to the presence of the Jew whether he was a peddler, a banker—or Disraeli, the nineteenth-century Jewish community's most famous apostate. Although the number of Jews was small and their wealth disproportionately distributed, they excited considerable interest. Some liberal Protestants worked with Jews to remove disabilities; the voices of anti-Semites, however, continued to be heard.

Jewish life in England was not controlled by ministers of the interior as it was in other European countries, nor were Jews ordered to change their religious practices in order to qualify for civil rights. Although Anglo-Jews found their lives easier than those of foreign Jews and although emancipation in England was basically unconditional, Jews struggled nonetheless. In their fight for equality during the nineteenth century, the challenge of anti-Semitism was met first by a political answer. When the Catholic Emancipation Bill passed in 1830, Jewish hopes for their own emancipation increased. Prominent Anglo-Jews joined with English liberals, such as Hazlitt, Macauley, Martineau, and Archbishop Whately, to insure the appearance before the House of Commons of a bill for the emancipation of English-born Jews. That bill failed, but Jews achieved other tangible political victories during the 1830s and 1840s. In 1831 trade restrictions preventing Jews from opening stores in the City of London were removed. In 1833 Francis Henry Goldsmid was unanimously called to the bar without his having to repeat in his oath the words, "on the true faith of a Christian."

David Salomons was elected Sheriff of London in 1835; Moses Montefiore succeeded him in 1837. Both took office without repeating those words of the oath. Salomons was elected an alderman of the City in 1836 but could not take his seat because in the City the oath remained. By an act of 1845, however, all municipal offices were opened to Jews. After 1845 Salomons served as an alderman; he became lord mayor in 1855. In Parliament, Jews met similar difficulties. Baron Lionel Rothschild, elected an M.P. for the City of London in 1847 and 1850, was unable to take his seat either time, nor could Salomons, elected an M.P. from Greenwich in 1854.[13]

The English argument concerning Jews' political emancipation was fought between those who favored a religious state and those who favored a secular state. The latter won in 1858 when the House of Commons modified its oath. The removal of disabilities made Jews eligible to sit only in the House of Commons, for the House of Lords did not modify its oath until 1866. Baron Lionel Rothschild, the first Jewish peer, sat in the House of Commons in 1865 and was admitted to the House of Lords in 1885.

Subsequent parliamentary bills removed remaining disabilities. While nineteenth-century Jews could attend Oxford and Cambridge, only after the passage of the University Tests Act in 1871, which remanded the universities' oath, could Jews matriculate for a degree. In that same year the Factory Act permitted Jewish-owned factories to operate on Sundays if they remained closed on Jewish holidays and the Sabbath. The Ballot Act of 1872 allowed Jews to vote in Saturday elections without religious transgression, by permitting Jews to cast their ballots before the Sabbath. With the passage of this act, the door to full participation in English life was completely opened. Jews could serve England and fully benefit from its institutions.

II *The Second Challenge*

In addition to facing the challenge of anti-Semitism, Anglo-Jews also had to cope with specific efforts made to eradicate Judaism through conversion. The Society for Promoting Christianity among Jews established by Evangelicals in 1809, took on the Christian responsibility for Jews' spiritual welfare.[14] During Victoria's reign, some forty branches of this society operated in England, attesting to the serious nature of their purpose and their threat to the Jewish community. (During the nineteenth century six separate missionary societies, formed specifically to convert Jews, operated in England; there were forty-three worldwide. The well-known SPCAJ was the longest lived.) Because Jews comprised a minuscule portion of the population in the early nineteenth century, attempts to convert them would appear disproportionate if ingrained anti-Semitism were discounted. Jews could not discount anti-Semitism; and the Evangelicals could not disregard the Jews, a people neither pagan nor Christian and living within a Christian society. Pamphlets and novels exhorting Jews to accept the true Messiah streamed from the presses.[15] In some of these, details of Jewish liturgy, rituals, and household practices indicate a fairly thorough knowledge if not a comprehension of things Jewish. Conversionists thus hoped to lure Jews to Christianity utilizing the Jewish religion. Even more potentially powerful were those tracts and novels written by Jews who had already converted to Christianity and who pressured their former coreligionists to join them.

Perhaps the earliest nineteenth-century conversionist novel was Amelia Bristow's *Emma de Lissau,* published in 1828.[16] This is a fairly sophisticated work, for the novel both exudes a Christian bias and includes authentic details of the Jewish household. While the characters in *Emma de Lissau* and in three other Bristow novels collapse under the weight of their creator's didacticism—a loud call for conversion—it was the first time the Jewish household was treated realistically if unenthusiastically. Bristow was probably the earliest conversionist writer, but she was not the first to write novels in which conversion was the theme. Maria Edgeworth was one predecessor. Called to account by a reader for her portraits of Jews guilty of treason, perjury, extortion, fraudulence, and murder, Edgeworth tried to compensate in *Harrington* (1816) by having her Christian protagonist react against his anti-Semitic education. He falls in love with a Jewish girl. But to his joy Harrington discovers at the last moment that the girl has been christened. She is Christian, not Jewish, and they can marry. This thematic handling is different from Bristow's. The latter highlights what she believes is the negative side of the Jewish religion to justify conversion. But Bristow did treat the Jewish household realistically. Moreover, she and Edgeworth introduced two other subjects for fiction about the Jew: conversion and intermarriage. As the nineteenth-century Anglo-Jew became more tolerated and accultured, fiction increasingly utilized these twin subjects.

Even a casual reading of Bristow's novels permits the reader to feel the vigorous challenge of conversionist literature. No statistics document the exact number of Jews converted by Evangelical efforts, but at least one school, the Jews' Infant School, founded in 1839, was established specifically to thwart conversion. Were the conversionist novels merely anti-Semitic, the threat might have been much less than it was when the novels in fact pretended sympathy and exploited an extensive familiarity with Jewish customs and beliefs. The Jews were being challenged on their own ground.

III   *The Third Challenge*

The third challenge Anglo-Jews faced arose within their own community: how to retain their Jewish identity in an essentially liberal social setting which encouraged them to acculture, that is, to emulate English values and mores (throughout, I make the sociological distinction between acculturation, a minority group's emulation of a dominant culture's values and mores, and assimilation, a minority group's absorption into a dominant culture). This problem became more identifiable during the last quarter of the century, for until 1858 Anglo-Jews concerned themselves with their political emancipation and then, for roughly two decades after that, with the Jewish community itself. The two early challenges by English society to reject Judaism were met with more confidence than the challenge from within. Ango-Jews tried to hold their community together. Early in the century the fight for emancipation had forged bonds of unity among Jews. Having achieved emancipation, Jews focused on providing communal services and integrating Jewish immigrants of varying backgrounds. These two interests as well as the community's concern for the welfare of foreign Jews reinforced earlier bonds and tended to keep the community closely knit. To the multiple community pressures, Jews responded positively. At mid-century the general pull of the community was to be Jewish. In the last quarter of the century, however, there seemed to be a spiritual disintegration as more Jews quarreled about Orthodoxy, married out of the faith to advance themselves socially, repudiated Judaism, or simply ignored their faith. To a much less extent Judaism lost children educated in English schools.[17]

Moreover, new waves of immigrants in the 1880s and 1890s kept the problem of differing impulses toward Judaism in the foreground. The challenge to be a good Jew, answered successfully by community work in the middle quarters of the century, was met by a more troubled and less unified response in the last quarter, as individuals struggled to define what being a good Jew meant. By 1897, while the immigrant was still enthusiastically religious, the anglicized Jew no longer supported or involved himself and his children in religious education, giving as reasons the inordinate time consumed, the inculcation of narrow-minded attitudes, and the use of Yiddish. To read Anglo-Jewish novels is to perceive that achieving emancipation and dealing with the community's institutions left Anglo-Jewry with internal tensions which appeared unresolvable. The pressures with which the community dealt successfully for two decades after emancipation provide an additional and more intense backdrop for understanding the novels.

The internal tensions felt by the Anglo-Jewish community during the last quarter of the century became obvious after the Jews' political emancipation. Removal of political disabilities in 1858 freed the Anglo-Jewish community to look after its internal affairs, primarily through revision of Jewish education, relief of the poor, and substantial reorganization of its community institutions. Until 1840 all Anglo-Jewish communities were to a large extent commercially and socially self-contained. Education of Jewish children, with the exception of those few who attended Christian schools, was provided solely by Jewish philanthropy. By 1850 there were at least four voluntary day schools in London and a few others in the larger provincial towns. These had a combined student population of

2,000, with only thirty-six teachers. From 1850 to 1870 the community opened new schools with lower student-teacher ratios and expanded the curriculum, which had previously included only the study of religion and the Hebrew and English languages. (English-language study was incorporated into the Sephardic schools' curriculum in 1735. The first authorized translation of a Hebrew prayerbook appeared in 1836; a Sephardic prayerbook, it was translated by D. A. de Sola. English was first incorporated into religious services during the 1840s and was restricted to sermons.)[18] Learning English history and literature enabled students to feel more comfortable in their adopted country and opened to them a wider range of jobs. While learning Jewish tradition, culture, religion, and Hebrew, the students were in fact being anglicized. Anglicization raised problems between parents and children who did not speak the same native language or possess the same traditions. It probably also led to the "dwindling Orthodoxy" lamented in some later novels.

Until 1871, to obtain a university education, wealthy Jewish students attended the University of London, founded by Isaac Lyon Goldsmid, a loan broker, among others. There were consequently only a few native scholars in the community; the best were immigrants from Russia and Eastern Europe. In 1845 Jews' College opened to train rabbis.

Whatever the educational level of its members, the community supported an Anglo-Jewish press whose rise parallels that of the Anglo-Jewish novel. It was born in 1835 with the founding of the *Hebrew Intelligencer,* a periodical which existed until 1840. 1841 saw the birth of two newspapers: the *Voice of Jacob,* which lasted until 1848, and the *Jewish Chronicle,* which continues to the present day. The *Jewish World* began publication in 1873 and rivaled the *Chronicle* in popularity for a while but merged with it in 1934.

Jews in England, like other disenfranchised groups, apparently devoted no time to writing fiction prior to the nineteenth century. Compelled to dedicate great energy to the defense and consolidation of their position after 1656, Jews restricted their literary activity at first to theological and philosophical treatises. Later, they wrote about social issues and translated the Bible and prayerbooks. Moreover, until the nineteenth century the novel was not a major art form nor a forum for expressing ideas. When the novel burgeoned as an art form, Jews began to publish fiction.

Although the population supported a press, it did not support its synagogues, at least by attendance. An 1851 census reports only 10 percent attendance at Sabbath services.[19] While this figure certainly reflects partial acculturation of the Anglo-Jewish community, it also reflects the general secularization of society during the period, paralleling the drop in attendance ratios at English churches. Nonetheless, following the pattern of movement of the middle class to the suburbs, in 1861 the Sephardim established a suburban branch of Bevis Marks, the original Sephardic synagogue, and the Ashkenazim established a branch of the Great Synagogue. The Jewish Reform movement failed to influence Anglo-Jewry as strongly as it would American Jews, but by 1840 a Reform synagogue, consisting of both Ashkenazim and Sephardim, was founded.

In spite of the growth of branch synagogues, attendance at religious services dropped. Nonetheless, Jews retained religio-ethnic loyalty, markedly in attention paid to relief of the Jewish indigent (for which Jews received grudging praise from non-Jews). Prior to 1881 immigrants were easily settled into the London community. Until the late 1850s approximately 200 immigrants a year arrived. During the 1860s this number increased to 300 and 400 a year, brought from Eastern Europe by famine, epidemics, pogroms, and conscription. From the 1850s through the 1870s, the Ashkenazim and the Sephardim of London acted in concert to provide for their relief, to find homes for them in the provinces, and to coordinate the needs of the various communities. To consolidate services to the immigrants and to suppress pauperism, both groups of Jews established the Board of Guardians for the Relief of the Jewish Poor in 1859. The United Synagogue, created by an act of Parliament in 1870, placed all metropolitan Orthodox synagogues under the Chief Rabbi. Under this organization the Sephardim and the Ashkenazim were closely linked, and cooperation of the two groups under the United Synagogue's umbrella extended to all the charitable agencies of the synagogues.

The voluntary consolidation of community institutions was one of the major communal achievements of mid-Victorian Jews. The other was the establishment of the Anglo-Jews as guardians of Jews in Eastern Europe and the Middle East. The move to protect Jews in other countries began as early as 1840. In that year the Jews of Damascus were accused of ritual murder. Their leaders were imprisoned, tortured, and sentenced to die. Moses Montefiore, then the head of the Jewish Board of Deputies, an early Anglo-Jewish political organization, secured their release. Subsequently, with the support of the English government, the Board of Deputies worked to aid Jews in Russia, Morocco, Greece, Persia, and Rumania. In 1871 the Anglo-Jewish Association, formed to protect foreign Jews and to intervene for their rights, relieved the Board of Deputies of that responsibility.

When foreign Jews emigrated to England, Anglo-Jews in London assumed responsibility for them. After the first wave of immigrants arrived in 1880, English Jews quickly grew dismayed with the East-End ghetto, transplanted as it was from Eastern Europe with its own language, newspapers, schools, and theaters as well as all its filth, squalor, and exotic smells. The immigrants clustered together because they were bound by a common social, political, economic, and religious tradition. In their new country they were bound even more closely by similar jobs and problems. Within one or two generations the immigrants would be acculturated to their new environment, but in the meantime Anglo-Jews were as repelled by these foreigners as were their non-Jewish counterparts for some of the same reasons and some reasons uniquely their own. For example, as Anglo-Jews acculturated, they became less Orthodox even if they did not formally become Reform Jews. As the formidable number of immigrants settled in London, Orthodoxy once more became preeminent, splitting native Anglo-Jews off from the newly arrived Jews even more than before. Less strict adherence to Judaism replaced Orthodoxy as the immigrants acculturated; but with each wave of immigrants this pattern repeated itself and stirred the community anew each time. Late Anglo-Jewish internal social problems, previously between Sephardim and Ashkenazim, became triangular. The older, virtually ethnic distinction proved longer lived, however. As the immigrants acculturated during the twentieth century, disdain and hostility died, but social distinctions between Sephardim and Ashkenazim remained and remain. Although the Anglo-Jews present a solidly unified front to their non-Jewish countrymen, in social matters their community is as deeply divided as it has always been.

With the exception of Israel Zangwill's short stories and his novel, *Children of the Ghetto* (1892), few of the changes made within the Anglo-Jewish community appear *directly* in the novels. Those published during the last quarter of the century, however, are clearly informed by the alteration in Jewish children's education, the difficulties besetting foreign Jews, and the influx of indigent immigrants. Moreover, the special problems attendant on one's Jewish identity receive particular attention. Many of the novels observe the

Anglo-Jew as he becomes accultured to English society. The novelists in general criticize acculturation, notably the move away from
Orthodoxy which, they believe, results in such fearful consequences
as intermarriage and apostasy. They see as another result of
acculturation increasingly widespread, mere nominal adherence to
Judaism, which permits the rise of the despised but prominent
materialistic Jew.

The novelists, despite their criticism, were also becoming accultured. Indeed, the overwhelming majority of Anglo-Jews wrote
about English, not Jewish, life. Of the forty-two nineteenth-century
Anglo-Jewish novelists I have identified, only fifteen wrote about
Jewish life or culture, and these not exclusively.[20] The fact that
Jewish novelists wrote more novels about English life than about
their own suggests that the issue and process of acculturation were
dominant concerns. They were also aware, however, of both positive
and negative portrayals of Jews in English works.

IV *The Jew in English Literature*

Historical anti-Semitism is reflected in English literature. Non-
Jewish writers before 1800 stereotyped the Jew negatively as a
murderer, traitor, or rapacious moneylender. The literary convention arose during the thirteenth century through histories, poems,
ballads, and dramas recounting the supposed ritual murder of Hugh
of Lincoln (twenty-seven versions are extant). In the medieval
mystery play the Jew-villain made his first dramatic appearance as
the red-haired, red-bearded Judas, as Satan, and as the sin of
avarice. The Jew as usurer, heretic, and ritual murderer had been a
well-established myth for two centuries when Elizabethans, with
their interest in the Bible, vitalized the stereotype in drama. Little
change was to occur for almost two hundred more years. The Jew
continued to be cast as a villain because of his religion, although
there were no known Jews in England.

In 1579 a play called *The Jew* was produced, first of a long line of
dramas with Jewish villains.[21] In *The Jew* the leading character, the
usurer, has Judas's red whiskers. By makeup, dress, occupation, and
later by speech, the stereotyped Jew would be recognizable. In
Marlowe's *The Jew of Malta* (1588) the Jew is a crafty merchant and
an assassin. Shakespeare portrays Shylock (*The Merchant of Venice*,
1594) as revenge-ridden and as a probable convert to Christianity,
but his character is also a tragic representative of suffering Jews. In

Fletcher and Massinger's *Custom of the Country* (1691) the Jew is a procurer. Dryden, in *Love Triumphant* (1694), portrays the Jew as an apostate. The first use of gibberish to characterize the Jew coincides with his delineation as a cowardly villain in John O'Keefe's *The Young Quaker* (1783). General Burgoyne's *The Heiress* (1786) was the first play to present the Jew as a fence. As a peddler and a broker, the Jew figured in melodramas of the nineteenth century, beginning with *Ella Rosenberg* (1807), by James Kenny. In these dramas the abstraction of the Jew as exotic, wealthy, cunning, and malevolent proliferated. For almost six centuries playwrights apparently catered to the popular view of Jews. And this view was not limited to dramatists. Novelists and poets saw the Jew similarly: as a shrewd, cruel, avaricious bargainer who rapaciously capitalized on his environment for monetary gain.[22] Gothic romances utilized the myth of the Wandering Jew. In the novels of William Godwin (*St. Leon,* 1779) and Matthew Lewis (*The Monk,* 1795), the Jew's hypnotic eyes gave him magical powers.

In the 1790s a change occurred. In 1794 Richard Cumberland countered the negative stereotype in his play *The Jew,* with Sheva, the benevolent moneylender and philanthropist, a characterization influenced no doubt by Lessing's *Nathan der Weise* (1779). The saintly Sheva, idealized and sentimentalized, fails to convince one of his Jewishness. In the same way negative stereotypes show the Jew superficially, so does Cumberland's positive stereotype. But an alternative to the negative stereotype was finally presented on the stage. Romantic poets sympathized with the persecutions Jews had suffered, but they wrote of the Jew primarily as a remote biblical figure. Regency novelists like Maria Edgeworth continued the stereotypic tradition begun by dramatists and denigrated the Jew as one from whom treachery, disloyalty, rapacity, and ritual murder could be expected. At the same time, Scott was interested in the historical Jew and produced in *Ivanhoe* (1819) the romanticized Jew, Rebecca, who was idealized as possessing intelligence and ability. Both stereotypes distanced the Jew, allowing him to be seen as evil or good but not as human. In drama the tradition of the Jew as villain was gradually replaced by that of the Jew as old clothes peddler, based on Jews of the poorer classes and used to provide comic relief. During the nineteenth century the stereotypes of the Jew in fiction altered as they were influenced by the changing perception of the Jew's position in English society.

CHAPTER 2

The Challenge from Without: Anti-Semitism

I *The Early Novelists*

EARLY Anglo-Jewish novelists such as Celia and Marian Moss were aware of the anti-Semitism and of the traditional as well as more contemporary negative English literary stereotypes—of the Jew as rapacious moneylender in Maria Edgeworth's *Belinda* (1801), as bogeyman in her *Harrington* (1816), as would-be seducer in Mrs. Frances Trollope's *A Romance of Vienna* (1838), and as avaricious fence—the personification of evil—in Dickens's *Oliver Twist* (1838). At the beginning of *The Romance of Jewish History* (1840), the earliest published Anglo-Jewish fiction, Celia and Marian Moss indicate their awareness of anti-Semitism. They state that "prejudice prevented [earlier] novelists from publication," but that in 1840 they could expect a fair judgment of their work.[1] These novelists were also aware of the idealized, sentimentalized Jews created by Sir Walter Scott in *Ivanhoe* (1819), whose noble exotic Rebecca possesses unsurpassed if somewhat magical knowledge of medicine and the art of healing, and Disraeli in *Alroy* (1833), whose eponymous protagonist rallies the Israelites and wins a nation only to lose it and his life after he marries out of his faith. Awareness of both kinds of stereotypes caused another early Anglo-Jewish novelist to complain: "The Jews are still considered aliens and foreigners; supposed to be separated by an antiquated creed and peculiar customs from sympathy and fellowship. Yet they are, in fact, Jews only in their religion, Englishmen in everything else."[2]

To meet the challenge of anti-Semitism, early Anglo-Jewish

novelists, as in the above complaint, argue on their adversaries' ground and in their terms. They capitalize on the historical novel to create sympathy for Jews and to allay English fears. Like Edgeworth, Mrs. Trollope, Scott, and Disraeli, they create stereotypes, but they also try to show that the Jew was not very different from the Englishman. They distance the Jew, showing him not in nineteenth-century England but in Egypt or medieval Spain. They attempt to arouse sympathy by depicting his historical suffering and unjust victimization; by stressing his persecutions, not his triumphs; his preternatural goodness, not his evil; his historicity, not his Gothic eerieness. They approach their English audience thus to ease English fears and gain for Jews acceptance or at least tolerance. In the face of community efforts to remove disabilities, these novelists felt less concern about the reception of their novels as literature and more concern for the sociopolitical position the novels might help their people attain.

II   *The Moss Sisters*

The women who are the earliest nineteenth-century Anglo-Jewish novelists, Celia (1819—1873) and Marian Moss (1821—1907), later Celia Levetus and Marian Hartog, ran a private school for some forty years. They were also poets and short-story writers as well as the editors of the short-lived *Jewish Sabbath Journal* (1855). *Early Efforts,* their sole poetical work, was published in 1838, a few years before they coauthored two three-volume sets of short stories and novellas: *The Romance of Jewish History* (1840) and *Tales of Jewish History* (1843). As Mrs. Levetus, Celia Moss later collected six of her own tales and published them in 1865 under the title *The King's Physician and Other Tales.* These examine the anti-Semitism Jews experienced in medieval Europe, England, and Spain.[3] The Moss sisters' response to the challenge of anti-Semitism is didactic. They cite as the impetus behind their fiction the desire to acquaint English readers with Jewish history, religion, customs, and to elicit sympathy for Jews of the present by writing about Jews of the past (*RJH,* Dedication), thus "explaining" the Jews to the English in much the same way Scott "explained" the Scottish to the English in *The Heart of Midlothian* (1818). To accomplish their ends the Mosses use the historical setting of the ancient Middle East, beginning with the Jewish year 2643, when the Jews were still an "independent people" (*RJH,* Preface). Collectively, their short stories and novellas are highly atmospheric, they have lavish palaces or tents, stark but clean hovels—and sentiment.

One typical novella, "The Storming of the Rock" (*RJH*, I), the Mosses set during the reign of King Saul, in the Jewish year 2673. A young, poor Jewish maiden, Judith, is captured by the Philistinian army leader, Amalek, who wants to make her queen of his harem. Kept in a richly adorned tent, Judith shrinks from Amalek's fierce desire. After the Philistinian king decrees she must be a sacrifice to their gods, Judith bravely thinks, " 'I can but die. . . . What matters if this weak flesh endures a few more minutes of torture than I reckoned on? He who cares for the meanest of his creatures, will give me strength to bear' " (*RJH*, I, 39). The Philistines prepare Judith by dressing her in costly robes with gold ornaments and precious jewels. She is brought before the altar while the Philistines wildly dance and discordantly pray to Dagon, their chief god. A sacrificial fire near the altar burns higher when a Philistine mother hurls her deformed baby into it. As Judith is led up the steps of the altar, the Hebrews advance, crying, " 'For God and Israel' " (43). They decimate the Philistines and rescue Judith.

The conclusion to this tale contrasts the harsh Philistines and the noble Jews. King Saul had sworn to put to death any Israelite who ate before the army fought the Philistines. His son, Jonathan, unknowingly eats some honey and is sentenced to die. The Israelite soldiers will not allow Jonathan to be executed because he preserved them from the Philistines. Saul accedes to their wishes. Through the two loosely joined parts of this story, the Mosses sentimentally and didactically teach that Jews are more noble and more high-minded than their enemies. They also picture the Israelites as merely a separate, ancient tribe. As such the Victorians could sympathize with these biblical Jews, who did not want to buy a house in their neighborhoods, without ever connecting the Israelites to Jews who were their contemporaries and who wanted to be part of English life.

In these weakly executed tales, Jewish historical background coincides only with dates and names of the biblical victor or vanquished. There is little attempt to explain the Jewish, Egyptian, or Christian cultures or the differences among them. The tales are backdrops for characters who act according to preestablished personalities. The Mosses present evil or unfaithful as well as noble or faithful Jews, a nonpartisan justice which permits them to moralize overtly. The differentiation into evil and noble Jews allows the

Mosses to indicate to their English audience that Jews, like Christians, can be good or ignoble. Evil Jews are sharp featured; they are proud, ungenerous, crafty, or effeminate, and may "violate the ties of nature," as does Absalom in "The Slave" (*RJH*, I, 69). These Jews are purged from the family or community, suggesting that the English reader need not worry: Jews will not allow evil deeds, committed even by their own, to go unpunished. In contrast, noble Jewish males are fine featured, wear pleasant expressions, walk with a firm step, and frequently, like Manasseh the armor-bearer, have an expression of "sadness . . . that accorded ill with [their] youthful appearance" (*RJH*, I, 17) when they must go to war. Female Jews are always noble. When threatened with torture or death (frequent occurrences), the timid weep; their stronger sisters throw back their long hair defiantly, then gaze stonily at their persecutors. Noble Jews receive a temporal reward. The men conquer their enemies; the women are rescued.

All antagonists of Jews are evil. Sinister Egyptians and, later, sneering Christians prey on Jews. Egyptians murder Jewish males and sacrifice Jewish women or use them sexually. Egyptians and Christians alike are evil, the Mosses argue, because they oppose Jews unjustly. The moral of each story underscores this point: faithful Jews ultimately overwhelm unjust non-Jews. Moreover, as in "The Pharisee" (*TJH,* II), some Jews are so noble that their example makes a Roman want to become a Jew. Of course he does not; the Mosses want to flatter their non-Jewish audience into sympathy, not frighten them into more hatred, which the conversion even of a Roman might accomplish. Nevertheless, the Mosses do chastise their English audience for their treatment of Jews. A narrative address complains that all countries, "England not excepted, hath treated us like a haughty mother-in-law does her step children, casting us forth from her bosom" and making Jews conceive of themselves as "sojourners in the land of the stranger" (*TJH*, II, 232–33). (Although the authors appear to speak for all Jews, most Victorian Anglo-Jews did not conceive of themselves as sojourners.)

Despite their overt criticisms of past persecutions, the Mosses' fiction was meant to flatter English readers for belonging to a society that believed in forebearance and tolerance: *they* operated no Inquisitional thumbscrew. Jewish custom is described, yet in deliberately vague terms, with a stress on its exotic Easternness rather than in any opposition to Victorian Christianity. Some rituals are explained, in footnotes which functon as direct addresses to the non-Jewish reader. Without any attempt to familiarize their English audience with the enduring elements of Jewish tradition and religion, the Mosses thus depict Jews as different in an inexplicable yet romantic way and set them in a remote past.

III   *Grace Aguilar*

Descendant of a family of Sephardic Jews, Grace Aguilar (1816– 1847), another early novelist as well as poet, translator, essayist, and short-story writer, was keenly aware of her English audience.[4] Six of her eight literary contributions which deal with Jews are nonfiction. In these, Aguilar seeks to explain Jews and Judaism to Christians, as she writes in the preface to her first book of short stories, *Records of Israel*, "in the hope that some vulgar errors concerning Jewish feelings, faith, and character may, in some measure, be corrected."[5] So successful was Aguilar that by 1844, according to one of her critics, she was known to her Christian public as an authentic spokesman for Judaism.[6] Although another critic allows that Reform Jews might claim Aguilar as a forerunner because she so frequently decried Jewish tradition, she was equally passionate in advocating knowledge of Hebrew for Jewish children (Abrahams, 142–43). Of her seven works of fiction, a volume of short stories (incorporating *Records of Israel*) and one novel focus on Jews. (Her other novels are either historical or domestic.) The volume of short stories, *Home Scenes and Heart Studies*, contains sketches of Jews in England and Spain. In those about Spain, such as "Josephine" and "The Escape," Aguilar presents the false reason—the charge of proselytizing—Ferdinand and Isabella used to banish Jews from Spain as well as the torture of a Marrano, Alvar Roderiguez, suspected of concealed Judaism. In "The Perez Family" she enables the Victorian reader for the first time to learn about Anglo-Jewish domestic life from the Jewish point of view. Set outside Liverpool, this tale illustrates the influence of English life on Jews.

Her novel *The Vale of Cedars; or, the Martyr,* written between 1831 and 1835, was published posthumously by her mother.[7] This novel concerns a Jewish girl who loves but refuses to convert and marry an English Catholic. She dies of torture inflicted by the Inquisition, and her beloved returns to England. Aguilar deftly exploits the historical novel to bring Protestants into sympathy with Jews after the Catholic Emancipation Act.[8] Had this novel about Jews in Spain on the eve of the Inquisition appeared during the thirties, Protestant readers would have been sympathetic to those who suffered at Catholic hands. Published in 1850, the year the Holy See was reestablished in England, the novel still commanded an anti-Catholic audience, and, by then, also appealed to English readers who were more sympathetic to Jews.

Perhaps Grace Aguilar used the historical novel because, as she wrote in the nonfiction *Women of Israel,* the true spirit of the Jews could not be ascertained from their "present State," which finds them socially and domestically amalgamated with peoples of lands in which they live. To distinguish Jews from the rest of the population, she complains, non-Jewish novelists create false portraits of Jews by calling a Jewish character "from the Past, when oppression forced upon him a particular character, and placing him in the Present, where he looks about as much out of place as a mail-clad baron and his rude-mannered suite would seem, in the luxurious and refined assemblage of England's present peers."[9] Aguilar correctly pinpoints one flaw of non-Jewish novelists' portrayals of Jews. In *Vale of Cedars,* she sets herself to redress their wrongs and "explain" the Jews to the English.

Aguilar shapes the plea for sympathy in *Vale of Cedars* through setting, characterization, and praise of the Victorian reader. The novel takes place in the Catholic court of Ferdinand and Isabella. There, aristocratic Sephardim who conceal their religion mingle gracefully—although, because of their concealed Judaism, somewhat uneasily—with Catholic royalty and courtiers. If Marranos implicitly receive praise for grace under pressure, so does their plight evoke sympathy. Moreover, Aguilar's characterization of Catholics as antagonists insures sympathy for ancient Jewish suffering. In a marked attempt to refrain from dividing the fifteenth-century world into good Jews and their malevolent oppressors, Aguilar presents good as well as evil Catholics. They can be differentiated mainly because the good Catholics advocate persuasive methods for converting Jews to Catholicism rather than torture. Yet they, too, are horrified by contact with one of the despised race, as when Father Francis learns that Marie Morales, the heroine, is Jewish: "Father Francis staggered back several paces, as if there were contamination in remaining by her side, and then stood as rooted to the ground, his hand convulsively grasping the crucifix which had nearly fallen from his hold; his lips apart, his nostrils slightly distended, and his eyes almost starting from their sockets."[10]

Good or evil, Catholic characters are uniform in their anti-Semitism, in suspecting Jews of using magic and sorcery to gain whatever unholy ends they desire, and in believing that Catholic souls will be damned by association with Jews.[11] The noble, suffering hero, Arthur Stanley, is also a good Catholic. (By making Arthur Stanley a Catholic whose birthplace is England, Aguilar provides variety and reinforces the idea that all Catholics cause suffering.) He loves Marie, but upon hearing that she is Jewish, "Arthur staggered back, relinquishing the hands he had so fondly clasped, casting on her one look in which love and aversion were strangely and fearfully blended" (20). Arthur continues to love her but believes his love arose through "the magic and the sorcery, by means of which alone her hated race could ever make themselves beloved" (77). He prays for Marie to become a Catholic and marry him; but the possibility of his becoming Jewish never occurs to Arthur. It should not, for his conversion to Judaism would weaken Aguilar's plea by suggesting overtly that Jews were Victorians' social equals.

Praising Victorians for their tolerance (of which Catholics were apparently not to partake) is another method by which Aguilar shapes her message. The narrator compares fifteenth-century Spanish Catholics and nineteenth-century Protestant Englishmen in passages that obliquely compliment Victorians for allowing Jews to live in England without concealing their religion and for their comparative lack of prejudice toward people regarded in less enlightened eras as "the scum of the earth" and "vermin" (28, 255). Protestant fears of Rome were certain to coincide with those of the Jewish narrator, whose own anti-Catholic bias springs to the foreground with comments such as the following about the Inquisition: "Its parallels [torture] will be found, again and again repeatedly, in the annals—not of the Inquisition alone—but of every European state where the Romanists held sway" (183).

Aguilar shapes her plea for tolerance through her insistence that Jews are different from English Victorians only in their religion. To minimize doctrinal differences, the narrator skims over actual practices, while highlighting their similarities to Christian customs. Thus, she never clearly defines Judaism. She never names Jewish holidays; instead, she identifies each by a roughly concurrent Christian holiday. Descriptions of rituals and customs are oversimplified and ignore spiritual meaning. She emphasizes the physical components of the ceremonies: the booth erected for the festival of the harvest, the interior of a temple, the marriage canopy under which a couple stands, and the natural setting of a Jewish funeral. An example is Marie's Jewish wedding. Features unique to the rite such as the use of the canopy, the lifted veil, and the broken goblet are merely noted in this exterior delineation:

[The Rabbi] stood within the portals, on the highest step; a slab of white marble divided him from the bride and bridegroom, over whom a canopy was raised, supported by four silver poles. . . . But so thick a veil enveloped [Marie's] face and form, that her sweet face was concealed, until, at one particular part of the mysterious rite . . . the veil was uplifted for her to taste the sacred wine, and not allowed to fall again. . . . The wedding ring was placed upon her hand—a thin crystal goblet broken by Ferdinand [the bridegroom], on the marble at his feet—and the rites were concluded. (47– 48)

Each description employs adjectives such as "peculiar" and "mysterious," which distance rather than reveal anything about the spiritual significance of Jewish practices.[12]

Similarly, prayers spoken in Hebrew are designated as prayers in an "unknown language" (114). Clearly the language is unknown to the reader and would be to a Christian observer, but it is known to the participants and to the author, who could if she would identify it. Aguilar uses Englishmen's own terms—"peculiar," "mysterious," "sorcery," "hated," and "unknown"—employed by some Christians to castigate Jews and Judaism. She gives these terms new meaning by showing that what is "peculiar" can also be deserving of praise. In much the same way, narrative pleas for spiritual charity present Judaism so as to erase distinction of belief and emphasize similarities between men, as when she requests, "Oh, that in religion . . . man would judge his brother by his own heart; and . . . as precious as his peculiar creed may be to him, believe so it is with the faith of his brother" (215). Like passages which compare fifteenth-century Spaniards and nineteenth-century Englishmen, these pleas could be accepted as praise by non-Jewish readers and as an additional way of perceiving Jews as similar to themselves.

Another way to see how Aguilar uses English terms is to compare a non-Jew's description of a synagogue with hers. In a letter of April 22, 1662, John Greenhalgh relates his impression of his visit to the first Sephardic synagogue in England:

At the east end of the Synagogue standeth a closet like a very high cupboard, which they call the Ark, covered below with one large hanging of blue silk;

in it are the Books of the Law kept. Before it, upon the floor, stand two mighty brass candlesticks, with lighted tapers in them; from the roof, above the hangings, two great lamps of christal glass, holding each about a pottle filled to the brim with purest oil, set within a case of four little brass pillars guilded. . . . Then the Priest arose and some of the chief Jews with him, and they went with a grave, slow pace, up the Synagogue, to fetch the Law of Moses, and when they came to the Ark wherein it was kept, the priest drew the curtain, and opening the double door of it, the Law appeared, then the whole assembly stood up and bowed down just toward it, and the priest and those chief ones with him, stood singing a song to it a little while. The Law was written in two great scrolls of very broad parchment.[13]

In *Vale of Cedars,* Aguilar, too, describes a temple as if through the eyes of one unfamiliar with Judaism:

Its interior was as peculiar as its outward appearance: its walls, of polished cedar, were unadorned with either carving, pictures, or imagery. In the centre, facing the east, was a sort of raised table or desk, surrounded by a railing, and covered with brocade. Exactly opposite, and occupying the centre of the eastern wall, was a sort of lofty chest, or ark; the upper part of which, arched, and richly painted, with a blue ground, bore in two columns, strange hieroglyphics in gold; beneath this were portals of polished cedar, panelled, and marked out with gold, but bearing no device; their hinges set in gilded pillars, which supported the arch above. Before these portals were generally drawn curtains, of material rich and glittering as that upon the reading-desk. But this day not only were the curtains drawn aside, but the portals themselves flung open . . . and disclosed six or seven rolls of parchment, folded on silver pins, and filled with the same strange letters, each clothed in drapery of variously colored brocade, or velvet, and surmounted by two sets of silver ornaments, in which the bell and pomegranate were, though small, distinctly discernible. A superb lamp, of solid silver, was suspended from the roof; and one of smaller dimensions, but of equally valuable material, and always kept lighted, hung just before the ark. (46–47)

Neither Greenhalgh nor Aguilar explains what is seen, Greenhalgh through ignorance, Aguilar through reticence.

Because Aguilar wants her readers to tolerate Jews in their difference without necessarily understanding them, she distances everything Jewish. To stress religious or ritualistic rationales might reveal or accentuate unacceptable differences. Better to avoid detailed religious explanation. If Victorians found themselves unable to understand Jews on a religious basis, perhaps they would understand Jews as people. Judaism could then be presented as a "peculiar" mystery; there would be no reason to include explanations of ritual. Differences between Jews and Christians, except to enlist sympathy for Jews by designating them Jews, would be secondary to the message for tolerance. Aguilar believes a Jew must remain a Jew, and she strongly deplores conversion to Christianity. Marie is "preserved from the crime—if possible more fearful in the mind of the Hebrew than any other—apostacy" (245). But Aguilar forecasts circumstances in heaven as entirely different. As Marie dies she tells Stanley, " 'In heaven I feel there is no distinction of creed or faith; we shall all love God and one another there, and earth's fearful distinctions can never come between us. I know such is not the creed of thy people, nor of some of mine; but when thou standest on the verge of eternity as I do now, thou wilt feel this too' " (248). Moreover, Marie blesses Isabella, knowing " 'we shall meet again, where Jew and Gentile worship the same God!' " (250). The Jewish idea of the hereafter is not defined in human terms, such as people meeting again. When we turn to Aguilar's nonfiction for explanation, we see a strong correlation between Marie's beliefs and Protestantism, which permeates the author's fiction and nonfiction.

The Jewish Faith (1846), a series of letters, reveals a young Jewish woman acutely aware of the difficulties of being raised in a predominantly non-Jewish environment. *Sabbath Thoughts* (1853) exposes her "admiration" for Christians and her worship with them to enlarge "an unprejudiced mind."[14] Abrahams suggests that *The Spirit of Judaism* (1842), edited with a restraining commentary by Rabbi Isaac Leeser, is permeated with the effects of her acquisition of Judaism by way of Christian texts (142). This was a difficulty not easily overcome because translations of Judaica into English by Jews were not readily available. Abrahams notes that Leeser published his translation of the Bible, the first in English and Hebrew, in 1845, only two years before Aguilar's death (143).

I am not suggesting that Aguilar moved toward embracing Christianity, rather that she was raised among non-Jews and that their influence becomes perceptible in the above-mentioned works as well as in the novel under discussion. Another critic, Philip Weinberger, asserts that Aguilar endeavored in all her works to teach Judaism and the role of the woman in Jewish history to her coreligionists. He finds her nonfiction prose strongly Orthodox in thought and influenced by her Marrano ancestry, but he admits in his individual studies of *Israel Defended* (1838), which when she translated she intensified in argument, and of *The Spirit of Judaism* that he discovers "little indication that our authoress found Christian values and doctrine distasteful or irrelevant" (35). Clearly, in *Vale of Cedars* Aguilar's prime impulse is a desire to defend and evoke tolerance for Jews and Judaism. She must guard herself against the charge of proselytizing. But Aguilar's Judaism is a Christianized version (possibly another reason for her exterior descriptions of Jewish rites). Pervading Aguilar's ficton and non-fiction, and witnessed by her six books on non-Jewish subjects, is an accultured consciousness.

Accordingly, and in marked difference from both the Mosses and later novelists who portray at least some Jews as evil, Aguilar idealizes all her Jewish characters in an effort to evoke sympathy as well as tolerance, particularly for Marie, exhorted as she is to convert to Catholicism and finally killed by Torquemada's Inquisition. (All of Aguilar's Jewish characters radiate nobility, gentility, and resolute faith—prepared for by Disraeli's *Alroy*.) From the beginning of the novel when Marie denies her love for the Catholic Stanley to its close when she blesses " 'God for every suffering which has prepared me thus early for his home' " (247), her devotion to Judaism never wavers. Persuasion, worldly temptation, and torture which leaves her arm a withered bone serve only to elicit Marie's steadfast loyalty to her religion. If Protestant readers could admire Marie's strength and fidelity, so too could they approve of her obedience to her father, whose word is law and whose religion in every detail is sacred and unquestioned. Marie possesses noble qualities Victorian parents generally wanted to see in their daughters. And acceptance of Marie would not be very hard, to judge from her complexion: "brunette when brought in close contact with the Saxon, blonde when compared with the Spaniard" (17).[15] If Marie maintained religious loyalty, obeyed her father, and was able to fit into Spanish society, perhaps Jews could fit into English society.

We cannot know if Aguilar's English audience reasoned in this way, but we do know the novel achieved wide popularity in Jewish and non-Jewish communities in England and abroad. By 1869 *Vale of Cedars* had gone through eleven English editions, by 1903 three more were published. The total number of English and American printings, exclusive of new editions, totaled twenty-nine by 1916 when the last appeared. Seven translations, the latest in 1939, have been made.[16]

The Mosses' work and Aguilar's novel directly address non-Jewish readers and suggest that Christians can profit by learning tolerance for other creeds (almost as a by-product, Jews can learn how necessary it was and continued to be for them to cleave to their faith). While the Mosses' appeal is simultaneously more overt—because it prefaces their fiction—and more limited, Aguilar's plea permeates her novel. If these novelists wanted their English readers to gain comprehension of the Jew's special plight, their reticence, together with their reliance on stereotypes, didacticism, and heavy-handed direct addresses, conspire against their purpose of inspiring sympathy and tolerance. What is more, although they use the context of the historical novel, which presents the opportunity for disguised and therefore palatable commentary on contemporary problems, these novelists ignore issues such as emancipation, which might offend their English audience. Like most propaganda fiction, these works are too heavily biased by narrative assertion and too lightly supported or developed through characterization. As a response to the Victorian's ignorance of or antipathy for Jews, these works fail to enlighten or broaden their concept of that "peculiar" people.

IV　*The Later Novelists*

In the face of anti-Semitism, early Anglo-Jewish novelists used the historical novel polemically to flatter and to convert the English reader. They used past persecutions Jews suffered to create sympathy and tolerance and delicately to remind the reader of Victorian anti-Semitism without offending him or her. Half a century later, Anglo-Jewish novelists also had to combat anti-Semitism, but because England's political climate had become more hospitable, they no longer had to use the indirect, stylized historical romance as a pretense, although settings in countries other than England could still effectively remove the sting of accusation. Instead, later novelists used their contemporary situation, one in which anti-Semitism flickered intermittently into a glow, notably in foreign countries but also in English social life. Even in 1876 George Eliot could say the "usual attitude of Christians toward Jews is—I hardly know whether to say more impious or more stupid."[17] Generally writing to a dual audience of Christians and Jews after mid-century, later Anglo-Jewish novelists examined Jews more critically, evincing concern about behavior which could prompt anti-Semitic responses. Victorian readers of various convictions about Jews could accept critical Jewish appraisal of Jews as reinforcement of their own views, but they could also see that Anglo-Jewish novelists recognized the need for change within their own community and on this basis could possibly be converted from anti- to philo-Semitism.

V   *Mrs. Alfred Sidgwick*

For forty years, Cecily Ullman Sidgwick (1855—1934) wrote under the pseudonym of Mrs. Andrew Dean as well as various other permutations of her own name. Beyond the fact that she says in her book about German domestic social customs, *Home Life in Germany,* she was "born and bred in England," nothing else is known about this Anglo-Jewish novelist.[18] Sidgwick published nineteen novels and one volume of short stories. All of her fiction describes the ways middle-class parents, Jewish or Christian, scheme to marry their daughters and sons to mates the parents or other relatives choose. The short stories, *Scenes of Jewish Life* (1904), and seven of her novels, each of which saw one English and one American edition, deal with Jews.[19] These works are set in England or Germany or both. Sidgwick's views about Judaism and anti-Semitism become clear in her fiction. She condones intermarriage under certain circumstances, but she condemns conversion. Her examination of anti-Semitism includes its presence in foreign countries, where she knows it to be of a more virulent strain than in England. In three of her later novels about Jews, Sidgwick's English Protestant narrator shows the treatment foreign Jews receive.

Her earliest novel about Jews, *Lesser's Daughter* (1894), illustrates Austrian anti-Semitism. Austria is a country, the narrator states, "where the Jews are openly reviled."[20] Austrians living in England bring their intolerance with them. The comparison of Austrian and English attitudes openly compliments Victorians' more genteel demeanor, specifically by showing an Austrian Catholic woman's behavior toward Jews in general and her husband in particular. Sidgwick studies anti-Semitism at length in this novel, the subjects of which are Lesser and Corona Breman's intermarriage and the effect of Corona's bigotry on their daughter's relationship with her father. At the end of the novel Lesser dies trying to protect his daughter from the man Corona wants for her son-in-law. Corona, the wife, "held aloof from her husband's people with a violence that in England is quite unusual" (35); "even London, so tolerant, hospitable, and quick of appreciation, could not teach her better. Her real objection to her husband was that he had Jewish blood in his veins" (52). Much before Lesser dies, Corona destroys her marriage with caustic comments about her husband and daughter, like "How can I be mother to such a Ghetto face?" (18). Her prejudice shimmers through remarks such as these like an impenetrable, evil mist.

In contrast, Sidgwick depicts English anti-Semitism in *A Woman with a Future*.[21] In this novel the English wife, Hesperia Troy, ultimately runs away with an American Jewish millionaire, Mr. Cassel. Hesperia's husband, Philip, loathes Cassel because of the latter's persistent attention to Hesperia, but Philip Troy is not an anti-Semite. An examination of Sidgwick's work allows us to see this novel as praising Englishmen's forebearance.

Similar to her method in *Lesser's Daughter*, Sidgwick uses characterization and narrative commentary in *The Devil's Cradle* (1918) to reveal the influence of anti-Semitism, this time in Germany, on an English Protestant narrator. *Devil's Cradle* focuses on the narrator, Karen, and her trip to Germany for a Jewish friend's wedding. Karen marries an aristocratic German who dies in a duel. Subsequently, at the beginning of World War I, she escapes to England and marries an American diplomat. Arriving in Germany, Karen discovers that aristocratic Germans like Wolfram von Hohenroda want to rid Germany of Jews altogether. When Karen marries von Hohenroda, he refuses to receive her Jewish friends, and when she joins these friends at a restaurant, he ignores all of them. Von Hohenroda's attitude influences Karen's; she suddenly realizes she should not "be sitting in a public place . . . surrounded by Jews."[22] Suggesting she would never act the same way in England, Karen excuses her attitude, "In England you could never feel as I did that afternoon in Reichenstadt and that shows you how impossible it is to live in a place and not breathe its atmosphere. You may not like what you breathe, but you are influenced" (110). Karen's friendship with her Jewish friends becomes more distant, but she remembers the difference between attitudes toward Jews in Germany, and those in England and America, "In England and America you accept people of Jewish blood much as you accept other people: on their merits. If you like them you make friends with them; if you don't like them you avoid them as far as you can. But the German point of view is quite otherwise. 'Jews! *Infame Schweine!*' " (174).

Sidgwick's use of a first-person narrator-character here permits a latitude absent in *Lesser's Daughter*. The third-person narrator of her

1894 novel compares Austrian and English anti-Semitism and concludes that the late-nineteenth-century Victorian is more tolerant. In *Devil's Cradle* while the same kind of comparison is drawn between Germany and England, the narrator also reacts to German anti-Semitism as it occurs. Because she experiences anti-Semitism at first hand, rather than flatly states her opinions, however, these opinions are not forced upon the audience and therefore carry more weight with the reader.

In contrast to Sidgwick's other narrator-characters, the Protestant English narrator of *Iron Cousins* (1919) is timid when she, too, experiences German anti-Semitism. Again, German ignorant intolerance is socially exclusive. Like *Devil's Cradle, Iron Cousins* examines an English girl's reaction to Germany and German anti-Semitism. Hired in England, Sally, the narrator, travels to Germany to become a governess to the children of a German family. She is wooed by a German but marries an Englishman after he returns her to England. In this novel, as in *Devil's Cradle,* the Jewish interest is secondary, but Sidgwick draws German bigotry clearly and pointedly. Sally's employer believes that Jews "like to have Christian dependents and satellites to whom they can be free-giving" and therefore superior; she haughtily announces when they meet, "I am extremely anti-Semitic."[23] This narrator remains neutral to pronouncements like these, thinking, for example, "I waited in silence and hoped she would change the subject because it was not the one in which I had any interest or could speak with feeling. I had read about Jews in the Bible and *Ivanhoe* and I knew the Davids [a Jewish family] and liked them, but I was neither the partisan nor the enemy of the race"(31). Sally fails as well "to take up the cudgels for [England]" (87), but she faithfully relates what she experiences and so defines for the reader another variety of German prejudice. The novel conveys no specific attitude about this narrator's passivity. Viewed in the light of England's (and other countries') refusal to receive Jews and so save them from extermination in concentration camps during World War II, her passivity forecasts later twentieth-century treatment of Jews.

A third-person narrator relates the story of Sidgwick's last novel, *Refugee* (1934), which follows Helga, a Jewish refugee from Germany. Mrs. Cone, an Anglo-Jew, spirits Helga out of Germany and proceeds to try to marry her to various men until Helga accepts a cousin. Sidgwick portrays a gallery of middle-class Jews in *Refugee.*

Social climbers like most of her German characters, the Jews escape Sidgwick's scathing descriptions of Germans and their manners. Anti-Semitism precipitates the action of this pre-World War II novel in which physical abuse of Jews, instead of merely bigoted statements, is described. Helga's father " 'died in a German prison. . . . They beat him cruelly and he died of internal injuries' " because he " 'took care of poor Jews and helped them out of the country.' "[24] In addition, "Christians who had served Jews were often reckoned as Jews and badly treated" (56). She shows the treatment of twentieth-century Berlin Jews to be different from the treatment of fifteenth-century Spanish Jews only insofar as Germans do not care to convert Jews, although *Refugee* is written too early to include more than scant foreshadowing of Hitler's 'final solution' to the Jewish question.

With the exception of the narrator of *Devil's Cradle,* who is at least aware of the poisonous air she breathes, none of Sidgwick's other characters or narrators challenges anti-Semitic attitudes or asks for sympathy for Jews. Later Anglo-Jewish novelists apparently felt more comfortable in England by the turn of the century, and while they may have chosen to compliment what English tolerance they saw, these novelists were very possibly more concerned with stirring their audience, Christian and Jewish, to action on behalf of oppressed foreign Jews.

Perhaps believing that anti-Semitism was waning by the close of the century or that it needed a last push, Sidgwick suggests that intermarriage without conversion, already a fact of English and Jewish life, could be a positive way to combat anti-Semitism—if the partners were compatible in other ways. Lesser Breman (*Lesser's Daughter*) finds only grief in his marriage to a Catholic because "the woman at his hearth considered him a pariah" (52). In contrast to Lesser, Mr. Theodore (*Grasshoppers,* 1895, another novel about the preparation of children for marriage) finds bliss in his intermarriage, owing to the pecuniary interests he and his wife share:

His father, Mr. Lazarus Theodor, a German Jew, had clung with strong attachment to the ways of his youth. The son was over-anxious to forget them. His father had left him a handsome fortune which he soon doubled by clever speculation. At the age of thirty-three he married an English girl. . . . Mr. Theodore thought that the youngest daughter of a half-pay major would be economical in her habits; but he soon found that his wife spent money as if life was hardly long enough to compensate her for the privations of her early years. Luckily, even she could not keep pace with her husband's knack of raking money into his own till. They were a very flourishing couple. Mrs. Theodore staunchly upheld her husband in his resolve to forget his foreign origin. They spelt and spoke their name as if it had been an English one, and they avoided those old acquaintances who would not remember to utter the initial consonants softly, and to affix a final e.[25]

The Theodores' marriage flourishes because both partners interest themselves in money, have little empathy with others, and invest themselves in obliterating traces of Mr. Theodore's Jewish-German origins. Mr. Theodore is the villain of *Grasshoppers* despite his infrequent appearance. If any inference can be drawn, it is that Mr. Theodore, also successful in driving his father's clever partner out of their firm without recompense and so to his death, is a Jew worthy solely of removing himself, even in name only, from Judaism.

Lesser's Daughter and *Grasshoppers* partially portray the kinds of unions described in nineteenth-century Anglo-Jewish nonfictional accounts of the community. Some Anglo-Jews repudiated Judaism as early as the end of the eighteenth century to advance themselves socially and politically. In a number of cases Anglo-Jews became apostates for love; such unions were generally composed of wealthy Jewish men and Christian women. Sidgwick's wealthy Jewish men repudiate Judaism for love and for social advancement, but they do not do so formally. In addition, Jews who left Judaism were mostly upper-class Sephardim, generally more ambitious than Ashkenazim.[26] Sidgwick's characters are Ashkenazim. This difference indicates that during the intervening century, Ashkenazim, as well, married Christians for love, as does Lesser Breman, or for social advancement, as does Mr. Theodore.

Other characters—Germans, not English Jews—also find happiness in intermarriage, but for nonmonetary reasons. Eugenie Gutheim, a young Jewish girl in *Devil's Cradle*, determines to intermarry "in order to get a footing in army society" (23). That her marriage to the German Eduard von Gosen may turn out like Lesser's is suggested at their wedding. His parents mutter "asides about *Juden*" (38) and one guest, a German count, deprecates the union, " 'Von Gosen has made an ass of himself. . . . Such a Jewess!' " (104). Without doubt, comments like these make the narrator remark drily, "The parent Gutheims were buying this privilege [intermarriage] for their daughter at a high price [anti-Semitic statements]" (23). Older Germans in Sidgwick's novels seem to be the most prejudiced; younger people work things out. No narrative comments report the state of the von Gosens' marriage, but they appear happy. Likewise in *Iron Cousins,* a Jew marries out of his faith and that marriage also succeeds. Frau Crefeld, the wife, was herself born of an intermarriage. She had nevertheless hesitated before "she consented to marry an Israelite. . . . She said that she had drawn a big prize in the lottery of marriage . . . and that if she had a dozen daughters she could not wish them a happier fate than her own" (72). Thus, intermarrying for social advancement or love, so long as neither partner converts and both are compatible, merits Sidgwick's approval.

On the subject of intermarriage Sidgwick departs somewhat from historical data about the Anglo-Jewish community. Most of her intermarried Jews—in *Grasshoppers, Devil's Cradle,* and *Iron Cousins*—are German; although Lesser Breman is English, he figures in an earlier novel. In turn-of-the-century England, one writer avers, intermarriage was on the wane. Israel Finestein ("The New Community: 1880—1918," *Three Centuries,* 86—179) asserts, without providing his rationale, that the Anglo-Jew lost interest in intermarriage at the same time he lost interest in Jewish education. Finestein cites the end of the century as the point at which intermarriage and thus assimilation began to die out. (By 1961, he believes, intermarriage occurs only in the upper classes of Anglo-Jewry.) If we accept Finestein's appraisal, the Anglo-Jewish novels depicting intermarriage, most of which were published around the turn of the century, describe a fading phenomenon. Perhaps this is the way to account for various narrative handlings, descriptions, and final acceptance of intermarriage after the issue ceased being so important to the community. The fact that intermarriage continued in the upper class, some members of which rose to that class during the last quarter of the century, indicates that novelists' interest paralleled the reality. The assimilation described in books about the community was not a prevailing tendency; nonetheless, segments of the Anglo-Jewish community, large enough to be noticed by the novelists, were losing their Jewishness.

Although Sidgwick naturally disapproves strongly of anti-Semitism—and suggests Jews could eliminate it through intermarriage—she reserves her sharpest criticism for Jews who convert to Christianity and for Jewish women who domineer their husbands. *Iron Cousins* portrays just such an apostate. Jewish Ernst Schlösser anglicizes his name, joins the Church of England, and demands that he and his Jewish bride be married in a church. The English narrator, amused by his search for status, concludes her description of Schlösser with an analysis of his behavior through which can be heard Sidgwick's disapproval: "All these views and arguments presented a new corner of the world to me, a corner in which you were not English by blood but ardently desired to be, partly from genuine affection for everything English and partly from a discontent with the realities of your origin that no doubt was snobbish" (12). Sidgwick reflects the desire of some Anglo-Jews to become more authentically English and, in yet another way, flatters her English audience. This English narrator provides for some Christian readers a reinforcement of their own views: one cannot erase one's heritage. Sidgwick's view of conversion is not to be confused with Orthodox Jewish belief; Orthodox Jews treated apostates as if they had died. Despite her unorthodox position, Sidgwick does ridicule the snobbishness of some apostates and, on the positive side, implies that superiority consists in accepting one's heritage.

Sidgwick also criticizes domineering Jewish wives, who appeared with frequency in Anglo-Jewish novels toward the close of Victoria's reign.[27] Sidgwick's concern about these women, like that of other Anglo-Jewish novelists, shows awareness of a segment of her community which could evoke anti-Semitism. In her last three novels she shows women stepping into a power vacuum because their husbands, interested in making money, are rarely home. These women run their homes efficiently but without any interest in Judaism. Instead of building a Jewish home or teaching their daughters how to run one, these wives rule their homes through tears, arguments, and other manipulative methods, as does Frau Gutheim who has "a row with the taxi-driver and the maid about muddy boots and [a] trunk" (*Devil's Cradle*, 17). All are characterized as stout (Frau Gutheim weighs "about eighteen stone," 17), dress expensively, and appraise all newcomers—including the English narrators—shrewdly. Not only do they manage their husbands as efficiently as they run their homes, but they uniformly persist in trying to control the lives of all those around them. Frau Gutheim, using her daughter's position in army society, tries to advance herself; Mrs. David (*Iron Cousins*) and Mrs. Cone (*Refugee*) shamelessly try to make matches for all the single women they know. These women's dominance is highlighted by the fact that, although their husbands are usually present when their wives act domineering, the men are usually silent as well. All Herr Gutheim can manage in response to his wife's outbursts is to look successively "mortified," "incredulous," and to sigh "gloomily" (58 –

59). The wives' dominance is not to be read necessarily as a
manifestation of unhappy marriages (although they show little
genuine interest in or love for their husbands and children), for
Sidgwick depicts little of their marital relations; moreover, Mr. Cone
appears to adore his formidable spouse. Their husbands seem to
exist solely as providers of financial support for their wives' clothing,
expensive dinner parties, and interior decorating. Sidgwick criticizes
these women through narrative tone, description, and even indirectly
through ridicule: they invariably fail in whatever they set out to do.

Sidgwick combats English anti-Semitism by setting intolerance to
Jews in other countries. By so doing she flatters the Victorian reader
as being above such intolerance and thus works to win him to the
Jewish cause on behalf of oppressed foreign Jews. She portrays
intermarriage with and without conversion, mirroring life in England and suggesting at the same time that some Christians could
leave negative feelings so far behind as to marry Jews. Sidgwick's
criticism of domineering Jewish women indicates her awareness of a
possible Anglo-Jewish community problem which, she may have
felt, was likely to elicit anti-Semitism.

VI *Isidore G. Ascher*

A native Scotsman who moved to Canada around the turn of the
century, Isidore G. Ascher (1835–1914) battles anti-Semitism in *The
Doom of Destiny* (1895). He wrote at least one play, two volumes of
poetry, and three novels, but about his life and career nothing else is
known. In *Doom of Destiny*, Ascher protests against the Christian
view of intermarriage and follows that protest with praise of Jews.
The Protestant narrator and heroine, Edith Craven, believes her
prejudice against Jews to have been dissolved by the "entertaining
and brilliant" Jewish lawyer, Israel de Mardo.[28] Despite her belief,
Edith refuses his marriage proposal because she actually shares her
aunt's bias against an "alien" as a husband. While Edith's uncle
argues that de Mardo's religion is his only "drawback," he spiritedly
praises Jews as "masters of the world" and excuses Jews' propensity
to amass wealth because "wealth like intellect helps to govern the
world" (61–62). He continues in their defense: "Were all Hebrews
of the day like the sons of our aristocracy, independent of pecuniary
circumstances, I am certain their potent brain-power would produce
great statesmen, writers, musicians, artists, and poets. As it is, in
proportion to their numbers, they have a great intellectual promi-

nence" (62). In this novel these are the only remarks about Jews, and the uncle's comments idealize all Jews, presenting a picture as untrue as those drawn by anti-Semites. The two women's negative opinion of de Mardo as a potential husband color the novel's attitude more heavily, referring as it does to the one Jewish character and reflecting what can be called genteel English anti-Semitism. Moreover, Ascher portrays de Mardo much like Edith's other suitors, without giving the young man any opportunity to show his brilliance or intellectual prominence. Ascher's attempt, through the uncle, to plead for Jews and so counterbalance the women's opinion, fails, and the reader is left wondering where Ascher finally stands.

VII *Samuel Gordon*

Samuel Gordon (1871–1927) emigrated from Prussia to London when he was thirteen. Nothing else is known about his life. A novelist, Gordon wrote at least one play, nine novels, four of which are about Jews, and three volumes of short stories, *A Handful of Exotics* (1897), *The Daughters of Shem* (1898), and *God's Remnants* (1916). His first two volumes of short stories were combined and published in 1902 under the title *Strangers at the Gate.* These are tales that illustrate the joy or grief Jews experience according to whether or not they live in conformity with Jewish law, as in "The Grandchildren." In this narrative two children leave their grandmother's corpse instead of properly burying her body. Running away, they believe her ghost pursues them. Instead of watching their step, they look behind, stumble into a swamp, and drown.

Beginning in 1900, Gordon wrote four novels about Jews. Unlike Sidgwick and Ascher, Gordon takes a strong stand against acculturation and assimilation. In each novel he repeatedly stresses that Jews must not yield to anti-Semitism, must not intermarry, must not convert. Instead, Jews should plow their energies into the Jewish community and remain separate from non-Jews. Gordon meets the challenge of anti-Semitism by flattering that portion of the English audience which believed Jews should not mix with non-Jews socially—and certainly not through marriage.

Like Sidgwick, Gordon deals with anti-Semitism in foreign lands. Just at the beginning of the twentieth century when there were a quarter-million Jews in England and when Parliament geared its energies toward passing a bill restricting immigration, he wrote *The Queen's Quandary* (1903) and *The Ferry of Fate* (1906) to portray contemporary anti-Semitism in Poland and Russia, respectively. The Polish attitude reveals no change from the fifteenth-century Spanish Catholic viewpoint portrayed by Aguilar: to be a Jew is to be damned. In *The Queen's Quandary* Catholics do not need the pretense of an Inquisition to eradicate Jews, however; nuns kidnap a Jewish child, Adrienne Letschinka, and raise her as a Catholic. Like Aguilar, Gordon shows Catholics as deserving condemnation for religious bigotry and thus aligns anti-Catholics with Jews. A type of secret Jew, Letschinka has lived in many countries and can validly express what she has found to be the world's opinion of Jews:

> "The world considers my race an empty shell, unfit and useless, ever since its kernel, the blessing of salvation, is supposed to have been extracted from it two thousand years ago. . . . And like all things of no value, we have been consigned to the rubbish heaps, so that, in order to justify the world's opinion, we might assimilate from them the qualities of vileness. And having been kept in contact with things which are unclean and of bad repute, is it to be wondered at that many—nay, the greater part—should doubt whether we have remained undefiled or not?"[29]

Through Letschinka, Gordon rails against anti-Semites, who, again like Aguilar's Catholics, fear contamination by Jews.

In much greater detail Gordon reveals Russian treatment of Jews, an anti-Semitism more self-indulgent but as superstitious and abusive as Aguilar's Catholics evince. Like the early novelists, in *Ferry of Fate* Gordon flatters Victorian tolerance. Russians believe Jews are as dirty and loathsome as animals, fit only to be "pack-asses" and "beasts of burden."[30] Even a Russian who is sexually attracted to a Jewish girl cannot resist flinging her at the ground after he kisses her. *Ferry of Fate* revitalizes the scapegoat phenomenon. The Governor of the Russian town in which the novel is set wants to kill Jews because they are " 'cursed parasites . . . blood suckers . . . draining us dry of what is best in us, our energy, our vitality [through] an insidious magnetism making the wealth of the country gravitate to them' " (174–75). So strongly does this man despise Jews that he willingly dies rather than " 'haggle for my life with a Jew' " (245). Whatever the Victorian biases against Jews, Gordon shows an extreme which forces the reader to consider his own attitude toward Jews.

When Gordon focuses on the welfare of foreign Jews, he is also concerned about apostasy, by which some Jews socially advanced themselves. Gordon shows that Jews cannot fully leave their religion.

Adrienne Letschinka lives royally as a Catholic but reverts to Judaism on her deathbed. Similarly, Baruch Volkman in *Ferry of Fate,* who leaves Judaism primarily for social advancement—rationalizing his actions on his idealistic belief that he can help his people more if he is not known as a Jew—also returns. By placing apostates in foreign countries, Gordon indicates that Anglo-Jews should not consider conversion. Gordon stands against Jewish apostasy as strongly as he does against a non-Jew's conversion to Judaism. In *Unto Each Man His Own* (1904), he portrays a young Protestant Englishwoman who converts to Judaism because she wants to marry Arthur Clauston, a Jew. Here, Gordon illustrates his conviction that heredity and environment determine religious affiliation; so frivolous a thing as love cannot obliterate one's ingrained faith. Accordingly, when Ellen Clauston realizes that her one fear—" 'the racial instincts in us may refuse to merge' "—has actually transpired, she leaves Clauston to live with a vicar so that her unborn child will not have to be received "into the covenant of Abraham."[31] Gordon strengthens his argument against conversion through his depiction of Clauston's flirtation with self-betrayal by even believing a true conversion could be effected. Divorcing Ellen, Clauston swears "to hold aloof from all those who had married out of the pale [of Judaism]" (272). Non-Jews should not be tempted to convert, Gordon demonstrates, for their original religious instincts will sabotage their efforts. Moreover, Jews must marry only other Jews if they are to live according to the faith of their fathers and find personal happiness. Gordon thereby offers English readers, who were willing to tolerate Jews but not willing to mix with them, a way to countenance the Anglo-Jewish presence: through separation of religious and social lives.

Gordon does not merely condemn anti-Semitism, apostasy, and conversion. He offers Jewish separatism as a solution to problems besetting Christians and Jews after the waves of immigrants reached England in the 1880s and 1890s. Immigrant Jews, although freed from pogroms and ghettoes, lived in conditions so crowded and dirty that indigenous Anglo-Jews believed they had brought those ghettos with them, and Christians saw the immigrants as a threat. In a 1901 study of London's East-End slum, an English writer's fear of Jews emerges sharply:

So long as the Jews remain an isolated and peculiar people, self-centered in their organization, and fundamentally alien in their ideas and aims, the rapid growth of their community can hardly be regarded with complete satisfaction. The more prosperous and successful they become, the more hostility and jealousy are likely to be aroused by their presence; and it is conceivable that they may develop into an actual source of danger.[32]

Were the Jews to concentrate on acculturing, this writer argues, they would be less of a threat, and Englishmen would not be anti-Semitic. Gordon conceives of Jewish separatism as a way to halt anti-Semitism, but his interest is not in Jewish acculturation or assimilation. He views Jews as necessarily separate because of their religion. From this perspective Gordon suggests Jews plunge their energies into the Jewish community to educate and improve the lot of fellow Jews and thus stop anti-Semitic feeling. Gordon develops his idea through two characters, Leuw Lipcott and Arthur Clauston.

The devoutly pious Leuw Lipcott (*Sons of the Covenant*, 1900) remembers and respects the promise he made as an East-End slum child: to aid poor Jews when he became wealthy. Moreover, he recognizes that Judaism may be endangered by assimilation. He believes that

there are hundreds, thousands of us who . . . have risen superior to their surroundings. They have emerged from the teeming struggling depths of their kindred in race, flattering themselves that they did so by their own native mother-wit, and sublimely ignorant that the capital they started with was their portion of the national inheritance, which our people had accumulated during the years wherein their oppressors thought they were beggaring them irretrievably in hope and health and the will to live. And thus few, very few, have returned to give tithe or tale of their success where it was due.[33]

To circumvent this drift of Jews, Lipcott continues his philanthropy but moves also at the end of the novel to establish a three-year technical training institute for working-class Jews. Lipcott envisions the graduates, educated and imbued with Judaism, helping to abolish the East-End ghetto by qualifying for a broader scope of occupations and subsequently by moving into better living quarters. He hopes thus to strengthen and unify the Jewish community through simultaneous separation from the English and a Jewish education. Clauston, after he divorces Ellen, aims specifically to prevent Jewish assimilation by bringing together younger, wealthy, less religious Jews and older, poor, Orthodox Jews. His book about Judaism makes one wealthy, pretentious, acculturated Jew for the first time " 'proud of having been born a Jew' " (314). Presumably, this man will donate money to aid Clauston's communal work. Through efforts like Lipcott's and Clauston's, Gordon suggests Jews will live better, more in accord with Judaism, and anti-Semitism will be stopped.

Another area of the Jewish community Gordon, like Sidgwick, sees as needy of attention is domineering Jewish women. Their attempts to control the lives of those around them wreaks more havoc in Gordon's novels than in Sidgwick's. Becky Diamond (*Sons of the Covenant*) illustrates the busybody, social climber, and henpecker. Looking for applause, Mrs. Diamond thrusts her unwanted presence into a neighbor's life; she applies for charity on behalf of a poor widow. Instead of receiving charity, the widow is "persuaded" to allow one son to be adopted. Later, the widow bitterly berates Mrs. Diamond. At least in this instance, Becky Diamond is partially motivated by humane concern for a child's nutrition (possibly becoming the archetype for the modern stereotyped "Jewish mother"), and Gordon acknowledges her concern. He does not condone her treatment of Mr. Diamond, however. Throughout the novel Becky Diamond maneuvers her husband like a puppet, leaving Mr. Diamond to console himself with the knowledge that "he would follow the call of the Destroying Angel instead of listening to the earnest importunities of Mrs. Diamond to keep where he was and continue to draw his salary" (423–24). He finally rectifies his deference to her temper, providing a model for dominated Jewish husbands to follow. Gordon thus asserts another way of improving the Jewish community and quelling anti-Semitism.

Through two later portraits in *Unto Each Man His Own*, Gordon shows what will happen if Jewish men do not control their women. Clauston's mother, Chaya Rachel Clausenstein, tries to manipulate Clauston by stubbornly refusing to accept Ellen, and she controls their home. (The portrait of Chaya Rachel may be a partial answer to the depiction of Anton Trendellsohn's father in Trollope's *Nina Balatka* [1867]. Both parents oppose their sons' choices of wives. Chaya Rachel prophesies that Ellen will be a "serpent" in Clauston's bosom (48); the elder Trendellsohn tells Anton he " 'will live to rue the day [he] first saw [Nina].' "[34] Chaya Rachel does not have the opportunity, as does Mr. Trendellsohn, to predict the division of her son from their people by his choice of a bride because Ellen, unlike Nina, converts to Judaism before she marries Clauston.) Although Chaya Rachel lives in her son's home, she marks out the kitchen as her territory: "her favorite position, whenever Ellen was in the house, was the doorway of the kitchen where she stood, a lynx-eyed sentinel guarding the stronghold of her gastronomic orthodoxy. The Christian girl might turn the rest of her house upside down, but the kitchen was, and would be, Chaya Rachel's" (78—79). Realizing too late that she loves Ellen, and guilt-ridden about her meddling, Chaya Rachel blames herself that Ellen has left, but she can heal nothing. Another domineering widow in the same novel is Mrs. Louisson. Causing even more severe damage with her attempts to control, Mrs. Louisson kills her husband. Although Mr. Louisson actually dies of a "trifling ailment," it "was but the best pretext he could find for dissolving their union with any show of decency" (6). Without a husband to manipulate, Mrs. Louisson turns her attention to her daughter's social advancement and almost succeeds in marrying the poor girl to a man she neither respects nor loves. Like Sidgwick, Gordon indicates the Jewish woman's need to learn control of herself. He suggests, through his younger characters like Lipcott and Clauston, that marital relationships will improve after Jews direct their energies toward the Jewish community.

Gordon ranges further than Sidgwick and Ascher in his depiction of Jewish beliefs, from Orthodox to Reform, and in his portrayal of the social workings of the Anglo-Jewish community, from poor through middle class. He is the only one of the three strongly to advocate the need for a Jew to be involved positively in the Jewish community. Sidgwick, Ascher, and Gordon feel less tentative and less angry about their situation in England than the Mosses and Aguilar but assuredly as concerned about Jews in England and foreign countries. The works of these three later novelists indicate that by the 1890s Victorians were aware of Jews, whether or not they liked Jews, and that they needed neither an historical introduction nor an explanation of rituals and customs, such as those provided by the early novelists. The three later novelists meet the challenge of anti-Semitism not by pleading for sympathy and tolerance, but by addressing themselves to specific, contemporary problems and offering equally specific solutions.

CHAPTER 3

The Challenge from Without: Appeals to Convert

THE second challenge to which Anglo-Jewish novelists responded was appeals to convert. Committed to the civilized eradication of Jews, the Society for Promoting Christianity among Jews worked tirelessly through any road it could open and some that appeared blocked. The psalmists took the course of religious appeal, composing hymns that ask God to bring the Jews to Jesus, as in "Great God of Abra'm! Hear Our Prayer" (1833):

> Great God of Abra'm! hear our prayer;
> Let Abra'am's seed thy mercy share:
> O may they now at length return,
> And look on Him they pierced, and mourn.
>
> Remember Jacob's flock of old:
> Bring home the wand'rers to thy fold:
> Remember too thy promised word,
> "Israel at last shall seek the Lord."
>
> Lord, put thy law within their hearts,
> And write it in their inward parts:
> The veil of darkness rend in two,
> Which hides Messiah from their view.
>
> Oh haste the day, foretold so long,
> When Jew and Greek, (a glorious throng,)
> One House shall seek, one prayer shall pour.
> And one Redeemer shall adore.[1]

Propagandists like Amelia Bristow took a more secular course, writing ponderous novels with a flavor of Judaism, that urged Jews to become Christians. In addition to Protestant conversionists who

55

wrote propaganda tales, Jewish apostates, frequently scornful of their former religion, proffered their efforts. Madame Brendlah, a Jewish convert to Christianity, authored *Tales of a Jewess* (1838), which is often vituperative in its conversionist stance.[2] Appended notes purport to explain Jewish rituals and customs but actually denigrate Jews and Judaism as foolish and superstitious. Denouncing the literary "mischief" perpetrated by false pictures of Jews— which, in *Women of Israel* she avows, actually fosters prejudice— Grace Aguilar criticizes such

narrations which portray some members of a Jewish family in a favorable light, that they may conclude by making them Christians, and the other members as so stern, harsh, and oppressive, that they bear no resemblance whatever to any Israelite, except the Israelite of a Gentile's imagination— [these depictions] do but swell the catalogue of dangerous because false works; and never fail to impress the minds of Christian readers with the unalterable conviction, that whenever spirituality, amiability and gentleness, kindliness and love, are inmates of a Hebrew heart, it is an unanswerable proof that that heart is verging on Christianity, and will very speedily embrace that faith. (309)

Those Christians who were not members of a conversion society, but who would have happily witnessed the conversion of the Jews, must have recognized assimilation to English life as another, perhaps less aggressive avenue to bring Jews to Christianity. Their reasoning for this hidden agenda might have followed a path like this: if Jews found themselves progressively accepted by Englishmen as they adopted the values and mores of English society, conceivably they would also adopt English religion. Although as prime minister the converted Disraeli was singled out as a Jew, conversionists capitalized on his novels to justify assimilation. Baptized at thirteen, Disraeli used his Jewish heritage in *Alroy* (1833) and *Tancred* (1847) to assert politically controversial ideas of Jewish superiority and separatism. These ideas, presented during the Jews' struggle for emancipation and rendered more significant by Disraeli's political power in 1847, stirred reviewers to comment. One critic, writing about *Tancred*, wants to see Jews assimilated to end the fallacy of English "religious and national prejudice" on the one hand and Jewish "extravagant national pride" on the other; employing with unconscious irony the situation of oppressed Russian Jews to support his position, he continues to plead for the assimilation of the Jews in England: "It is a good sign, that the persecution of the

Jews, even in Russia, is taking the character of amalgamation rather than of distinction; and that the violence of that unscrupulous government is now exercised to assimilate the Jews in costume and political duties to the rest of the population."[3] A far cry from Disraeli's philosophy, this critic's position on assimilation is a mere step from the conversionist's.

Small wonder, then, that Grace Aguilar berates conversionists, particularly Amelia Bristow, for distorting Jews, Jewish rituals, and Jewish family life, for, by

placing the scene in *England,* and in the present era, the author gives an imaginary picture of the *Polish* Jews, at least one or two centuries back, and containing not the very smallest resemblance to *English Jewish* life of the present age; in fact, there is nothing to write concerning Anglo-Jewish life in the present age. With the sole exception of the ordinances of their creed, their households and families are conducted exactly on the same principles as English households of the same standing. (314)

But some Anglo-Jewish novelists disagreed with Aguilar, believing that the conversionists' threat demanded a response in fiction. While the community answered the conversionists by founding Jewish schools for young children and by disseminating information about Judaism through the Anglo-Jewish press and cultural societies, the novelists' answer portrayed contemporary Anglo-Jewish life while exhorting Jews to remain Jewish.

I   *Charlotte Montefiore*

Charlotte Montefiore (1818–1854), a niece of Sir Moses Montefiore and the wife of Horatio Montefiore, was primarily a political and social essayist.[4] Montefiore's *Caleb Asher* (1845), probably the first Anglo-Jewish novel addressed specifically to Jews, argues against conversion at a time when the London branch of the conversion society was active. This novel, published simultaneously in England and America, concerns the problem of conversionists who gave poverty-stricken London Jews money as an inducement to convert. Montefiore's appeal to the Jewish audience is made through depictions of devout Jewish families which pervade the novel and through characters who discover that they cannot give up their heritage. Through the representation of Jewish rituals that assumes knowledge in the reader, the address to a Jewish audience is clear. Formal Jewish rituals are portrayed in two scenes. Obviously in accord with Orthodox practice, rituals in *Caleb Asher* are not explained as they would be for a non-Jewish reader: an apostate's family, forbidden even to mention his name, treat him as one already dead; having reverted to Judaism and dying, he praises the unity of God. Moreover, when the apostate Reuben Simeon reaffirms his Judaism, in a direct appeal to the Jewish reader, he emphasizes, without explanation, the Jewish God's unity, Judaism's moral base, and the 613 commandments which structure the way an Orthodox Jew is to live:

"Cling with all your heart and soul to the Divine religion, that proclaims THE UNITY OF GOD, which enjoins the worship of one God alone, and whose practices are all in accordance with this belief, a religion which the simple may comprehend and follow, which enforces love to God, charity and good-will to all men—whose moral creed contains no exaggerated enthusiasm, but noble and pure precepts that can be fulfilled letter by letter, and whose accomplishment gives peace here, and peace hereafter."[5]

In these scenes Jewish practice appears without externalization. No adjectives such as "peculiar" or "mysterious" describe the rituals. A non-Jewish reader might wonder why an apostate's family considers him dead and would probably ascribe it to social rather than religious practice, but the death-scene prayers make obvious the difference between the praise of one God, as opposed to a trinity, without the novelist's resorting to comparisons. In addition, those scenes in which the Jewish families are portrayed together depict these poor Jews as nourished by Judaism. Through the warmth of the religious atmosphere, Montefiore shows that Judaism is itself a nourishing force, knitting families close together.

Like the Mosses and Aguilar, Montefiore positions herself even more solidly against the blandishments of missionaries by dividing her characters into noble, self-sacrificing Jews and their materialistic Protestant oppressors. The major characters are the eldest sons of two Jewish families, Reuben Simeon, who converted before the story opens, and Caleb Asher, who contemplates conversion. They are followed in their respective situations. Reuben converted because his mother was reduced to penury. Reuben had received money for his family's needs from a wealthy female missionary until he became entirely dependent upon her. Then, she threatened to withdraw her aid unless he converted. With no other way to help his family,

Reuben joins and works for the London Missionary Society. Realizing he does not believe in Christianity and cannot formally convert, Reuben despairs because he has left Judaism. Caught between two religions, Reuben endures his dishonor and his remorse, believing he must die alone and without God because he bartered his faith for gold. Caleb decides to convert because he, too, can no longer support his family. Reuben saves Caleb from becoming a member of the Operative Jewish Converts' Institution, and Caleb repays the favor by helping Reuben return to his religion and family.

If the plight of these poor Jews is not enough to command the Jewish reader's attention to his own religious adherence, Montefiore shows that Christians active in the Institution are materialistic busybodies. The prime desire of the members of the Operative Jewish Convert's Institution is to make money for the society and converts to Christianity. The avowed purpose of this society is to "study to be quiet, and to do your own business, and work with your own hands, that ye may walk honestly towards those that are without, and that ye may have lack of nothing" (62). Despite the promise "to do your own business," members of the Institution give money with strings attached and sanctimoniously congratulate themselves. Like Aguilar's evil Catholics, these characters perform their duties for the church but are piously self-aggrandizing. Montefiore urges Jews to remain Jewish not only because they will find spiritual fulfillment but also because Christians fail to be truly interested in Jews' welfare.

Montefiore does not believe that all Christians are evil or that Jews should remain entirely separate, but subscribes to the philosophy that Jews should not proselytize. Parallel to the treatment of Jews by the members of the conversion society is the treatment of other Christians by Jews. Caleb befriends a widowed Christian mother and her child. Relations between the two families show how real friendship between Christians and Jews can be attained:

The widow and her little boy attend regularly to the forms and precepts of their own creed, and never was a word uttered by any of their friends to induce them to abandon it: but they often, together, talk of God; of his goodness to man; of his constant love; and they find that real friendship and harmony can exist between Jew and Christian, that religion even is a bond between them, and that whilst both look up to the Universal God, as to their common Father, they, as his children, must consider each other as brethren, and as brethren live together in peace and love. (102–103)

Comparing Jews and Christians, the narrator praises Jews for their lack of interest in proselytizing, a practice actually forbidden to post-biblical Orthodox Jews. Montefiore argues that Anglo-Jews must remain steadfast in their Judaism, but she includes Christians as friends in her model.

Although it is a didactic tale, Montefiore's narrator remains silent on the subject of conversion. No direct address cajoles or admonishes the Jewish reader. Her argument is structurally based on scenes in which family and friends demonstrate concern for each other, a concern which she shows is a major part of Judaism. Characters argue with each other, express opinions, and work through their problems. Any merits possibly to be found in conversion, at a time when Jews continued to be barred from work on the sole basis of religion, are not considered. Only through characters' actions and their consequences are readers cautioned against conversion. Montefiore's appeal to her Jewish audience is structurally different from Aguilar's narrative pleas to her non-Jewish audience for sympathy. Montefiore probably handles her appeal in such a manner so that it appears less of a sermon to poor Jews whose faith in their God did not fill their stomachs. In *Caleb Asher* Montefiore had the occasion to educate poor Jews to job opportunities available in 1845. Instead, as evangelical Methodist works of the period often do for their poorer Christian audiences, she preaches adherence to Judaism as the sole remedy for poverty, presumably because the threat of the conversion society was so great.

II   *Matthias Levy*

Matthias Levy, under the pseudonym of Nathan Meritor, wrote articles about the London Symphony and books on shorthand and Shakespeare. Levy wrote his only novel, *The Hasty Marriage; A Sketch of Modern Jewish Life* (1857), which went through one edition.[6] Nothing else is known about him, not even the years of his birth or death. Like Montefiore, Meritor addresses his novel to a Jewish audience and exhorts Jews to remain Jewish. Unlike Montefiore's cautionary appeal to poor Jews threatened directly by the conversion society, Meritor concentrates on more comfortable middle-class Jews and demands that they remain Orthodox in the face of what he views as a more subtle threat, that of assimilation. Meritor discounts conversion, stands squarely against intermarriage, and admonishes Jews to learn their own religion and teach it to their children. This kind of education, he believes, is the only defense against the disappearance of Judaism.

Because Meritor perceives Jews as more threatened by their emulation of English social and cultural mores than by any formal agent for conversion, he is not content, as Montefiore was, to place his diatribe solely in characters' mouths. Instead, in his twin-pronged attack on the Protestant church and irreligious Jews, Meritor harangues his audience by direct addresses, which he warns in the Preface are interspersed throughout. In fact, Meritor's prefatory comments are reiterated by one character, Edgar Lavite, the author's norm, as much as by his own direct addresses, but each of Meritor's points—against conversion, against intermarriage, and against irreligious Jews—is already enuciated in the Preface.

In *Hasty Marriage* Meritor endeavors to save Jewish "families from disgrace and children from ruin" as well as, first of all, to condemn conversion by questioning "the purity of Christianity [for, although it] is the boast of missionaries, the church is ready and willing at all times to receive into its bosom strangers, who believe neither in a Trinity nor the New Testament" (ii—iv). In this instance, the author's prefatory comments are reinforced by Edgar Lavite, the character whose example Meritor plainly wants Jews to follow. Lavite denounces apostates, especially those who maliciously ridicule Judaism, as partially responsible for anti-Semitism, for those who leave their faith are lured, Lavite declares, only by the promise of money. Lavite heaps his scorn on apostates' religious ignorance:

"Did you ever know a man change his religion from a sincere conviction and conscientious knowledge that the form of worship he was about to embrace was better than the one he was leaving? . . . Never! Would you tell me that a man who, from infancy, has been following the tenets of our religion, who has . . . faithfully and truly adhered to its precepts and doctrines . . . can suddenly, without any motive whatever, discover that the religion which it has taken him so many years to understand, is not the correct one, but that the religion which he has not studied for an hour . . . is the only one which can bring him to the desired haven?" (33)

Along with the criticism of apostates is a corollary attack on the Protestant church's blind willingness to accept converts.

Meritor also criticizes the Protestant church's lax rules about intermarriage because he sees intermarriage as equal to conversion in causing Jews to stray from Judaism. In his Preface Meritor presents the church's negligence as another reason for writing *Hasty Marriage*:

to bring clearly before the eyes of our authorities, as well as the authorities of other religions, the facilities which are afforded to Jewish girls, the temptations which are held out to them by the church, and the brilliant prospect . . . set before their eyes, and which induce them . . . to enter the marriage state, contrary to, and in defiance of, divine law. . . . It is an incontrovertible fact, that a Catholic and a Jewess, aye, a Mahomedan and a Unitarian, may be married in the church. I am willing to admit that the parties so married cannot be very ardent followers of *any* religion; nevertheless, if Protestantism is to be made the common receptacle for the refuse of other religions, then, I consider I am justified in calling into question the purity of the Trinity. That it affords the facilities for those kinds of marriages, one of which forms the turning point of this narrative cannot be doubted, and I consider, in thus attacking the principle, I am perfectly justified. (iii—iv)

Meritor repeats this diatribe later in a direct address and simultaneously enjoins the church to "institute the same rigid enquiries into the moral character of both parties prior to marrying them, as Judaism does" (129). The tirades against the Protestant church occur, with the exception of Lavite's denunciation of apostates, in narrative addresses to the Jewish reader, as if Meritor wants Jews who know Christians to pass on what he says.

Meritor's second attack is on irreligious Jews. By irreligious Jews, Meritor actually means Reform Jews, or as he calls them, "Reformers," who, he believes, raise their children negligently and actually cause them to convert or to intermarry. The relatively new Reform movement began in Germany in the 1820s. By 1840 a Reform synagogue, established by Sephardic and Ashkenazic Jews, prospered in London. To the Orthodox, Reform Judaism defies the established traditions of Judaism because in adapting itself to the times it removes many religious restrictions, shortens or fails to observe certain festivals, and ignores many traditions and customs. Some Orthodox Jews consider Reform Judaism a drive toward assimilation; *Hasty Marriage* implicitly shares this view. Seventeen years after the Reform synagogue's establishment in London, the narrator of this novel labels "Reformers," with their "flimsy ideas" and their "unsound and unstable doctrines" (27), harmful to themselves and Judaism, for, as "example is better than precept, and is . . . certain to be imitated, the children grow up in the opinions of their father which . . . do not gain anything by the change from orthodoxy" (8—9). Jews who become part of the Reform movement are certain to assist conversionists in helping Judaism to disappear, Meritor holds.

His assault on Reform Jews is conveyed, for the most part, by characters' beliefs and actions. Lavite, who functions as a positive example for adherence to the most stringent form of Judaism, pursues Meritor's argument. Lavite believes Reform Judaism to be a step away from no religion. Although "his religion taught him to revere and respect other religions" (79), Lavite dislikes Reform Jews because

their main object was to make religion subservient to their own convenience. . . . Their religion was an airy nothing with a local habitation; but while it lasted, it did harm. It sowed dissension, created discord. . . . took some from the orthodox faith; and it left a vague and uncertain impression on their minds; and . . . did the same amount of injury as it had expected to do good. (77—78)

Lavite observes Orthodox strictures and frequently tries to show a Reform Jew, Mr. Montague, that he is failing his children.

The Montagues illustrate Meritor's contention that children raised as Reform Jews experience little real religion and therefore lack a guide for moral living. The description of Montague's casual faith is immediately followed by a description of his flaccid effect on his children. Montague

could conform to the mode of worship he most admired . . . without any great harm to himself. . . . [But] there appeared to be less sincerity in his [Judaism], than in that of the general body of [Jews]; and this difference was not lost on his children. They noticed it; they followed in his footsteps. (9—10)

Montague goes so far with his Reform ideas that he can find an excuse for young people to leave Judaism. Consequently, the reader is not surprised when one of Montague's daughters, having fallen prey to his religious ideas, loses respect for her parents:

For her religion she cared nothing: and when that is the case . . . honour, affection, obedience, love—all, all are gone. . . . For religion being the fly-wheel . . . where that is not, the rest of the machinery is a nullity. It becomes useless; it gradually rusts, and ultimately rots, leaving a few dry bones to tell what might have been. And so with Caroline Montague. (24—25)

Caroline's disrespect for her parents is engendered by her ignorance of Judaism: "to Caroline, religion was a blank; she knew it not, consequently she had no guiding star" (130). Her ignorance leads her to marry her Catholic music teacher and later to a degraded life as a singer, two mistakes Meritor insists would have been avoided had her parents been Orthodox Jews. Reform Jews fail to instill the proper religious and moral instincts in their children. These children then defy their parents and convert or intermarry.

Meritor's concerns in *Hasty Marriage* are to indict the Protestant church, to caution Jews who may or may not be thinking of becoming Reform about that group's apparent insincerity, and to warn them of the consequences—which occurred in one instance of which he knows and formed the reason for this tract. Aside from the character of Edgar Lavite, narrative rhetoric and negative example shape the novel's dual argument. Meritor's handling is markedly different from Montefiore's. Whereas Montefiore embeds her argument in her characters' rhetoric, Meritor reiterates his points in the most obvious ways. A possible reason for their differing techniques may be Meritor's emotional involvement with the problems (an involvement affirmed in the preface and the novel), while Montefiore's more objective treatment could stem from her lack of emotional involvement or her desire to keep personal emotion exterior to her novel.

Another difference between the two works lies in the treatment of family life. Montefiore capitalizes on family scenes. In contrast, Meritor portrays less family life and almost no family closeness, thus illustrating further that Montague's neglect of faith and of rituals provides his wife and children with few occasions to be together as a family and finally sunders family ties. One Sabbath dinner is mentioned, but no feeling of family or rituals enters the scene which provides the occasion for Lavite to speak against conversion. His speech has little to do with the novel and appears to be included as another admonition to Jews who contemplate becoming Reform. Later on, at Lavite's wedding, family and rituals are again ignored, but Lavite's pious thoughts as he stands under the wedding canopy are emphasized. Montefiore in *Caleb Asher* includes more rituals, but to Jews who have experienced similar occasions ritual detail is not necessary. In *Hasty Marriage* the lack of familial togetherness at such times is noticeable and reinforces the thematic insistence that Reform Judaism destroys families.

Both novels address the Anglo-Jewish community about contemporary problems. Montefiore addresses poor Jews and urges them to resist the lure of the conversionists. Meritor harangues the comfortable, middle-class Jews who were converting as they advanced socially. Meritor's remedy, too, is Orthodox Judaism, unquestion-ingly followed. Although his novel is overt propaganda, Meritor first sounds the alarm for a problem which increased during the century. More than a few middle-class Jews obviously were willing to adapt themselves to "modern lights" (78), as Meritor feared in 1857, for later Anglo-Jewish novels, especially those treating the poor East-End Jew, lament Orthodoxy as "dwindling."

III   *The Later Novelists*

That conversionist efforts continued throughout Victoria's reign is apparent from late Anglo-Jewish fiction. Little change in conver-sionist methods appears, at least from the novelists' point of view. Oswald John Simon, a later and very minor novelist shows that Catholics and Protestants still threaten Jews. However, there is some change in the way Anglo-Jewish novelists met the challenge of conversion. Early novelists specifically addressed Jews; later novel-ists (Gordon, in *Queen's Quandary*, and Simon) addressed Jews and Christians but continued to deal openly with the subject. Only Benjamin Farjeon, in *Aaron the Jew* (1894), portrays an Orthodox Jew capable of withstanding conversionists' attempts. Moreover, Farjeon adds a quasi-scientific reason to the argument against conver-sion.

IV   *Oswald John Simon*

Oswald John Simon (1855—1932) shows a less subtle method used by conversionists than do Montefiore and Meritor. A champion of Jewish causes, Simon publicized East European Jews' difficulties. One of his articles, about the stages of Anglo-Jewish emancipation, appeared in the *Jewish Chronicle*. He was the son of Sir John Simon, a founder of the Anglo-Jewish Association.[7] His only novel, *The World and the Cloister* (1890), which saw one edition, is indebted to George Eliot's *The Spanish Gypsy* (1868), which shows a gypsy child reared by Catholics. In *The World and the Cloister*, the Catholic Duchess of Boughton undertakes the responsibility for rearing a Jewish child, Irene, but delivers her instead to a convent. Irene resists Catholicism, discovers her heredity, and indignantly confronts the duchess, who "willfully deprived me of my highest privilege, the knowledge of my kinship with God's selected band, and robbed my widowed mother of her only child!"[8] Her superior warns Irene as she leaves the convent, "You are going to spiritual destruction" (I, 267), but other Catholics, excluding the duchess, accept Irene's decision. Reunited with her mother, Irene studies Judaism and prepares for her marriage to a Jewish man. The duchess remains unrepentant of her act, continuing to be ambitious for Catholicism.

Like Montefiore, Simon employs no narrative address to the reader, but like Aguilar and Gordon, Simon accuses Catholics of evil acts against Jews. His Catholic characters conspire against Irene even after she unravels the mystery of her birth. Through the duchess's lack of repentance, Simon indicates that Jewish children continue to be endangered, for the duchess will presumbably continue her ruthless attempts to procure converts for her church.

V Benjamin Farjeon

Montefiore, Meritor, and Simon assume culture and tradition as the reasons for one to remain Jewish. Benjamin Farjeon (1838–1903) suggests that religion is in each individual's genes. (Biographical information on Farjeon can be found in Chapter 4.) In *Aaron the Jew*, through his protagonist, Aaron Cohen, Farjeon claims that adherence to a particular religion is an hereditary instinct; "it is in [the] blood."[9] Aaron Cohen, a building contractor by profession and a philanthropist by commitment to Judaism, is an Orthodox Jew who remains steadfast in his belief. Because Aaron is widely known in London as a charitable man, the Society for the Promotion of Christianity Amongst Jews solicits him "to assist [men whose commitment to Judaism wavers] in the praiseworthy task of examining their consciences" (267). Aaron, of course, does not believe in conversion. He prefers to see Christians and Jews strengthened in their respective religions: " 'Instead of endeavouring to convert Jews or Christians to a faith in which they were not born, would it not be better to employ ourselves in the effort to make those who call themselves Christians true Christians, and those who call themselves Jews true Jews?' " (267). Furthermore, he insists to the fund-raiser that religion is in the blood:

"Once a Jew, always a Jew, whether he follows the Mosaic laws or disregards them. So powerful is the seed of Judaism that it can never be entirely destroyed in the heart of one born in the ancient faith. We who are Jews know this to be incontrovertible; you who are Christians may not be able to understand it." (269)

Aaron's concept of "the seed of Judaism," for him an ineradicable part of a Jew's heredity, ignores the influence of environment; for Aaron, environment can have no effect on religion.

To prove to the fund-raiser his assertion that one cannot lose his original religious instincts, Aaron illustrates with the example of the Borlinski cousins. The Borlinskis are converts of whom the society is so proud that it now employs them to make other converts. Aaron first draws from the solicitor the information that it took two years of the society's monetary support before the cousins converted. Then Aaron reveals how the Borlinskis cleverly extorted money from "several [Jewish] benevolent institutions" (271) before Aaron unmasked them. Finally, Aaron proves his assertion "once a Jew, always a Jew" by the example of one of the Borlinskis:

"He believes, as we all do, in a future state, in the immortality of the soul. The White Fast is the great Day of Atonement, when Jews pray to be forgiven the sins they have committed during the past year. The most ignorant of them believes that if they pray and fast on the Day of Atonement their transgressions are atoned for. We have our black sheep, as you have; but the blackest of them observes this day with superstitious fear, and Josef Borlinski is not an exception. This year, on the Day of Atonement, I myself saw Josef in synagogue, enveloped in the white shroud he brought from Poland, beating his breast, and praying for forgiveness for his sins. From sunset to sunset he prayed, and grovelled, and trembled. Come to our synagogue next year, and you shall see him there, if before that time he is not called to his account. Though he be converted to twenty different religions, and baptized twenty times over, Josef Borlinski is a Jew, and will remain a Jew to the last hour of his life." (275)

(The Borlinskis appear only in others' conversations, but the reader learns that they shrewdly use their false status as converts for monetary gain, in effect becoming a Jewish joke on the conversion society.) Not only does Aaron believe that Jews should not convert, he believes they cannot.

Aaron's belief extends to Christians and underlies his major religious and moral problem, one which deals with conversion of a sort. Disapproving of intermarriage, Aaron faces a dilemma when his daughter, Ruth, wants to marry a Christian. Ruth, secretly adopted by Aaron to save his wife's life when their infant daughter dies, is actually a Christian. Although Ruth has been raised as a Jew, she has resisted learning Hebrew, going to synagogue, and has shown "an aversion to Jewish society" (322). All this occurs, Aaron knows, because "[Christianity] is in her blood" (322). Aaron's discomfort intensifies with Ruth's determination to marry, for Aaron believes that by raising her as a Jew, he has "violated the canons of his religion" and "robbed a young girl of her birthright" (324). To add to his moral discomfort, Aaron has felt his wife's pain over Ruth's attitude:

Ruth's dislike of Jewish society was not new to her [mother, Rachel]; it had caused her great pain. . . . Frequently and anxiously did Rachel ask herself, From whom could a daughter of her blood have inherited views and ideas so antagonistic and rebellious?

Aaron could have answered this question, had it been put to him, and had he dared to answer. Ruth's instincts were in her blood, transmitted by parents he had never known, and of whose characters he was ignorant. Heredity lay at the root of this domestic misery. As a rule, vices, virtues, and all classes of the affections are hereditary, and the religious sentiments are no exception. (285)

Judaic tenets rescue Aaron, Farjeon indicates. Aaron tells Ruth and Rachel the truth about what he did and frees Ruth to marry and live as her religious instincts demand.

Like Montefiore and Meritor, Farjeon stands against conversion to Christianity, but his protagonist is not even tempted by conversionists. Unlike the earlier novelists, he lends quasi-scientific credence to his argument by placing the cause for religious instinct in one's blood. Farjeon's treatment of the problem is somewhat similar to that of Maria Edgeworth in *Harrington* (1816), in which a couple is able to marry when the young woman discovers she is not in fact a Jew but a Christian. Unlike Edgeworth, Farjeon is obviously not anti-Semitic. He shows the Jew at his most honorable, loving his wife, desiring to save her life by presenting her with a live baby, atoning through the years for his deceit, and finally disclosing the truth. Aware that he writes for a dual audience, Farjeon appears less concerned with Christians' ideas about converts and more interested in undercutting attempts at conversion by describing religious affiliation as racial, as an inherited instinct. Like Simon, Farjeon is indebted to George Eliot. He reverses the situation of *Daniel Deronda* (1876), in which Daniel, a Jew, has been raised as a Christian. In this non-Jewish but sympathetic handling of the problem, the assumption of hereditary religion is made in Daniel's vocational uncertainty and his instinctive attraction for Mirah.

For whatever reasons they advance, culture, tradition, or science,

Anglo-Jewish novelists meet their second challenge, that of the conversionists, by admonishing Jews to cleave to Judaism. Simon and Farjeon examine conversion without the preaching, propagandistic techniques used by Montefiore and Meritor. Nor do they plead for tolerance or sympathy as the Mosses and Aguilar do, despite the fact that they address a dual audience; each could have seized the opportunity to plead following anti-Semitic outbursts which ensued subsequent to the arrival of so many immigrants to England in the eighties and nineties. In contrast to the cautious early novelists, these writers take a stand, criticizing or applauding without fear of offending their audience.

CHAPTER 4

Changing Views of the Anglo-Jew and the Novels of Benjamin Farjeon

THE convention of portraying the Jew disparagingly was about 600 years old when Richard Cumberland first countered it in his play *The Jew* (1794) with the figure of Sheva.[1] So saintly that he routinely thinks of others before himself, Sheva became the paradigm for the good Jew in the nineteenth-century novel. Cumberland's portrayal was followed by Edgeworth's of Mr. Montenero, Israel Lyons, Simon the Jew, and Jacob the Jew in *Harrington* (1816). Here, she apologizes for her earlier anti-Semitic depictions with three honest Jewish merchants and a professor of Hebrew. Transforming the good Jew stereotype into a woman, Scott created the noble Rebecca in *Ivanhoe* (1819) and Zilia in *The Surgeon's Daughter* (1827). Two of Scott's immediate imitators, Charlotte Anley (*Miriam*, 1826) and Horace Smith (*Zillah*, 1828), portrayed similarly noble, pious women. Equally noble if not pious are Leila in Bulwer-Lytton's *Leila; or, the Siege of Granada* (1838) and Leah in Du Maurier's *The Martian* (1897).

A romanticized Jewish male appeared in 1833 when Disraeli projected in *Alroy* a Jewish hero who championed Jewish causes. Variations of this stereotype appeared throughout the century. A representative list includes Disraeli's contemplative financier, Sidonia, in *Coningsby* (1844) and *Tancred* (1847); the contemplative intellectual, Raphael Aben-Esra in Charles Kingsley's *Hypatia* (1853), Hall Caine's Israel Ben Oliel in *The Scapegoat* (1891), and Sir Walter Besant's Emanuel Elveda in *The Rebel Queen* (1893); the generous Jew, Charles Reade's Isaac Levi in *It Is Never Too Late to Mend* (1856), Charles Lever's Ignaz Oppovich in *That Boy O' Norcott's* (1869), and George Meredith's Sigismund Alvan in *The*

Tragic Comedians (1880); the exaggeratedly virtuous, long-suffering Jew, Charles Dickens's Mr. Riah in *Our Mutual Friend* (1864); and the Jew who is compassionate and concerned about other Jews, Trollope's Anton Trendellsohn in *Nina Balatka* (1867) and George Eliot's Daniel Deronda and Mordecai Cohen in *Daniel Deronda* (1876). These qualities may have been present in some Jews, but such stereotypes indicate little attempt, except in the case of Eliot's characters, to delineate the Jew primarily as a human being. Eliot's *Daniel Deronda* is the only nineteenth-century novel which treats Jews, at least the minor characters, as complex human beings. Even Eliot was not completely successful; for, in the context of anti-Semitism, she did not avoid a counterbalancing special pleading.

Although novelists were creating positive types, the negative stereotype, that of the Jew as villain, also flourished throughout the century. Most negative portrayals were far more memorable than the idealized creations. For example, Edgeworth, Dickens, and Du Maurier first exploited the convention in the novel. Then, called to account by their readers, they tried to repair the damage with more positive depictions, but their evil Jews lasted far longer and were far more convincing than their pallid creations. One critic calls Dickens's Fagin (*Oliver Twist*, 1838), whose viciousness vividly appears in plays and movies based on the novel, a "prehistoric fiend, an aging Lucifer whose depravity explains him wholly" (Rosenberg, 118).

The negative stereotype commands our attention here because it is the one to which Anglo-Jewish novelists reacted. This stereotype altered three times during the nineteenth century; each time, the novelists answered with corrective types of their own. At the beginning of the century, the Jewish villain of the drama, target for hisses and boos, became a comic figure—a peddler or an old clothes man. Here he remained, with increasing tolerance softening later productions. Maria Edgeworth portrayed a number of Jewish villains, beginning in 1801 with her *Moral Tales*, stories in which the Jew is a traitor or deceiver. As a distrusted moneylender he appears briefly in Ann Radcliffe's *Gaston de Blondeville* (1825). As the Wandering Jew, following the tradition set by Matthew Lewis's *The Monk* (1796), he reappears in John Galt's *The Wandering Jew* (1820) and George Croly's *Salathiel* (1828).

By 1837 the Jewish fight for emancipation was underway, and the polarized attitudes common to emotional arguments inevitably gained newspaper space. While some sketches were sympathetic, common to the negative attitude were articles and poems which satirized the old clothes peddler as well as the leaders of the Jewish community and which called overtly or covertly for persecution. In addition, newspapers played up the activities of Jewish criminals. One of the most infamous and elusive of the London fences was Ikey Solomon, whose career spanned the years 1827—1831, when he was caught and deported to Australia. Newspaper references thereafter kept him in the public eye and helped prepare readers for Dickens's Fagin, the pimp who tries to corrupt Oliver Twist and the master-mind of London's criminal underworld.[2]

Early Anglo-Jewish novelists tried to overcome these negative attitudes and portrayals. Depicting heroes and heroines close to Scott's ideal, the Mosses and Aguilar counterbalanced negative portrayals with sentimentalized stereotypes. At least one early Anglo-Jewish novelist, Samuel Phillips (*Caleb Stukely*, 1842—1843), completely agrees with the negative stereotype, perhaps because he himself despised the lower-class Jew to whom he was bound by religious ties. Phillips depicts the Jew as a crafty, dishonest money-lender (see Chapter 6).

With the emigration of more Jews from Central and Eastern Europe and with the growth of London and its Jewish population (a large part of which was prosperous by this time), mid-century Victorians became more closely acquainted with the London Jew because they now encountered him more frequently in daily life—as a pawnbroker, clothes peddler, or perhaps even as a pimp or a small-time criminal. Parliamentary debates over Jewish emancipa-tion and articles about Jews and Judaism by Hazlitt, Macauley, Martineau, Archbishop Whately, and George Eliot, to name a few, provided for the expression of strong pro-Jewish sentiment. Nonethe-less, earlier literary antipathies continued with Thackeray ("Cod-lingsby," 1846; "Rebecca and Rowena," 1850; and *The Newcomes*, 1855), who delineates the Jew as a greedy exploiter and social invader; Bulwer-Lytton (*My Novel*, 1853), who depicts the Jew as a dishonest businessman; Charles Clarke (*A Box for the Season; A Sporting Sketch*, 1864), who portrays the Jew as an unscrupulous but comic moneylending lawyer; and Tom Hood (*The Lost Link*, 1868), who offers another unscrupulous lawyer, a thorough rascal with a lisp. Mid-century familiarity brought with it a new characterization: while retaining his crafty, rapacious qualities, the fear-inspiring Jew, even when grotesquely caricatured, became more human; dirty, poor, scornful of other Jews, he lisped or spoke a broken, comic English, a foreign gibberish which no longer had sinister overtones, as in "Codlingsby," *The Newcomes,* and *The Lost Link.*

Mid-century Anglo-Jewish novelists thus faced a new task: to rehabilitate the old clothes man, to deny that all Jews were dirty, poor, and spoke peculiarly. Most Anglo-Jewish novelists attempt to show that the Jew is "just like us," different from the Victorian Englishman only in his religion. Far from despising their coreligion- ists, these novelists prefer to stress the "Englishness" of the Jew, presenting him generally as a product of the middle class in manners if not in wealth. He speaks English correctly; he is concerned about his wife and family; his home is neat and clean; his occupation is that of scholar or honest businessman. In Meritor's *Hasty Marriage,* Edgar Lavite, an honest businessman and a pious Jew, chooses a wife carefully to insure the perpetuation of Judaism in his home. Intellectually prepared to discuss contemporary issues such as conversion, Lavite respects others' religions and rights while he remains a proud and honest Jew, able to take his place in the Jewish and English communities. Lavite thus functions as a counter to the negative stereotype.

In the last third of the century, when exploitation in English society was more in the hands of the financier than the manufac- turer, when commerce and industry became more international than local, when, in fact, the House of Rothschild held its head high among less Levantine companies, the Jewish international banker and speculator became an important stereotype. Seen as an unscru- pulous businessman at least since 1853 in Bulwer-Lytton's *My Novel,* the Jew was also stereotyped, notably by Trollope (*The Eustace Diamonds,* 1872; *Phineas Redux,* 1874; *The Way We Live Now,* 1876; *The Prime Minister,* 1876), Cecil Clayton (*Azalea,* 1876), and Du Maurier (*Trilby,* 1894), as a vulgar, insensitive boor, avaricious, cunning, exploiting Christians and fellow Jews, and trying to invade English society. In addition, the late influx of Jews from Europe during the last two decades of the century added a new threat. Poor Jews who spoke no English crowded together in the unsanitary East- End ghetto. They could not easily obtain jobs because of their lack of skills, inability to speak the language, and religious strictures. Nevertheless, the majority eked out a living in sweat shops and, some Englishmen believed, threatened to ruin the native English- man's chance for employment.

For the Christian writer the nineteenth-century Jew was, then, either paragon or archetypal criminal, the latter having a hall of mirrors six centuries long to reflect his image. The expanse between the poles had not been charted, although by the close of Victoria's reign a few hesitant steps had been taken. Early in the century the Jew in drama became a comic figure. In poetry from Byron (*Hebrew Melodies,* 1815) to Wordsworth ("The Jewish Family," 1828) to Browning ("Holy Cross Day," 1855; "Rabbi Ben Ezra," 1864; *The Ring and the Book,* 1868—1869; "Jochanan Hakkadosh," 1883) the Jew was portrayed more sympathetically, although as a biblical figure far removed from nineteenth-century England. As the Wandering Jew his image also changed. Gothic romancers kept him a doomed man but permitted him the capacity to perform good deeds as he wandered. In 1894 the Wandering Jew was revived as the master-hypnotist, Svengali (Du Maurier, *Trilby*). Although little except the power of his evil eye links him to earlier incarnations, he is strongly reminiscent of the odious archetype. In popular fiction the Jew continued to appear in historic or romantic form as well as in any of the varied, but familiar, villainous guises. By mid-century, though, Jewish characters had ceased to look alike. There was even some interest in internal disputes between the Sephardim and the Ashkenazim, based on the heavy Sephardic support of the Ashkenazic community and on the growing impetus toward Reform Judaism. In novels glances were cast at contrasts between the two groups (Frances Trollope, *A Romance of Vienna,* 1838), exploitation of Jew by Jew (Charles Lever, *That Boy O' Norcott's,* 1869), and the social exclusiveness of the Sephardic Jew (George Meredith, *The Tragic Comedians,* 1880). By the end of the century, the receptive reader could recognize that the character of the Jew had altered and broadened.

Despite positive changes in attitudes toward Jews, the later Anglo-Jewish novelists were forced into a third readjustment in response to the changing public image of the Jew. They now had to correct the overwhelming impression of the wealthy Jew as a rapacious, immoral boor and of the immigrant as a threat to the English workingman. Of all the later Anglo-Jewish novelists, Benjamin Farjeon particularly sets himself to correct unfaithful portrayals, notably the negative stereotype of the last third of the century. To do so, Farjeon concerns himself with language Jews supposedly speak (a component of the stereotype from the middle third of the century), anti-Semitism, and the figure of the Jew as businessman and family man. Most important, in 1875 Farjeon is the earliest Anglo-Jewish novelist to begin exploring contemporary Anglo-Jews' problems and to continue depicting different types of Jews. By so doing, Farjeon actually created the genre of the Anglo-Jewish novel.

Benjamin Farjeon (1838—1903) was a native Anglo-Jew of North African origin. His birth date is commonly given as 1833, but his daughter Eleanor states that her father was born in 1838, a year after Victoria was crowned.[3] Farjeon's parents were Orthodox Jews, and in their home in London's East-End area of Whitechapel Jewish ritual was strictly observed. At seventeen Farjeon travelled to Australia where, until 1868 when he returned to England, he was the editor and part owner of the first daily newspaper in New Zealand. Although Farjeon married an American Protestant and assimilated to English life, he did not convert. His daughter notes,

Pap was a devout believer without a creed. Though he was never seen in Synagogue, he remained a Jew by instinct, as well as by race; the Jews were proud of and claimed him, and in their organs condemned his marriage to one who was not a Jewess. But though this disbarred him from giving his children his race, he gave them the rich inheritance of his blood. Their "Christian" mother taught them her artless prayers; he told them tales from the Old Testament; and that was all their home-religion amounted to. (179—80)

Although Farjeon neglected to practice his religion and his children had no connection with the Jewish community, he remembered Jewish opinion of conversion and intermarriage and considered them in two of his four novels about Jews, *Aaron the Jew* (1894) and *Pride of Race* (1900).

Farjeon's assimilation to English life may also be seen in the fact that he wrote only four novels about Jews. A popular, prolific novelist from 1868 until he died, Farjeon wrote over fifty novels, several short stories, and one play. His novels with Jewish characters did not command the wide appeal of his two outstanding successes, *Grif* (1868), a story about Australian life, and *Blade-O-Grass* (1871), a novel about London slum life. *Grif* went through at least seventeen editions by 1898, *Blade-O-Grass* seven by 1899. Encouraged perhaps by his success with these two novels, Farjeon undertook to refute the still-existent negative stereotype.

In Farjeon's earliest novel with a Jewish character, *At the Sign of the Silver Flagon* (1875), he directly chastens writers like Thackeray ("Codlingsby," 1846; *The Newcomes*, 1855) and Tom Hood (*The Lost Link*, 1868) who depicted Jews as speaking gibberish. In *The Lost Link* the unscrupulous, moneylending Jewish lawyer, known only by the name of Levinson, speaks with a lisp which reduces him to a comic figure: " 'If ye va'ants to talk about bishnish, talk away and look sharp,' said Levinson. 'Ma time's precious, and I've clients to meet vith. Can't come here to talk about dogsh. Tishn't bishnish— tishn't bishnish, ye know.' "[4] Against jargon like this, Farjeon remonstrates:

It has hitherto been the invariable rule in English fiction to represent a Jew as speaking a kind of outrageous jargon, which has its source only in the imagination of writers who are either prejudiced or not well informed upon the matter. It is time the fallacy was exploded. The English Jew speaks as good English as an English Christian does. The "S'help me's!" and the "Ma tears!" and the "Vell! vell! vell's!" which in English fiction and on the English stage are set down as indispensable in the portrayal of an English Jew, are ridiculous, and to a certain extent mischievous perversions of fact. They do not belong to the very lowest class of English Jews, who, as a rule, speak their language much more correctly than English costermongers.[5]

He goes on to broaden his protest:

The English complain, with justice, that they are never properly represented upon the French stage; the English Jews may, with equal justice and equal truth, assert that their position in English fiction is a much more gross caricature than the representation of the typical Englishman in a French theatre. (63—64)

Silver Flagon, published four times in London and once in New York between 1875 and 1877, provided Farjeon a broad platform from which to correct English portrayals of Jews' speech.

Farjeon writes with authority about the speech of English Jews, for he grew up in the East End of London where immigrant Jews lived. Although two of his novels about Jews are not set in London's East End, all four depict Jews who come from poor families, who are generally devout Jews, and who speak English without the trace of an accent. Farjeon's authority, moreover, is reinforced by sociological facts. Immigrant Jews, arriving in England, settled first in the East End to live near Jews of their own class and habits. Approximately two hundred immigrants a year came to England until 1881 when pogroms and other factors drove a wave of Jews to England and other receptive nations. Because he arrived in smaller numbers, the immigrant Jew who came before 1881 could—if and when he did learn English—speak it with more facility than he is sometimes presented in English fiction as being capable of for several reasons. Like the small number of Jews who arrived prior to the Victorian period, he was likely to be more easily settled in England than the large number of Jews who arrived together after 1880. Although adult English language classes began only in 1892, the immigrant was eager to speak English because facility with the language enabled him to be part of English life and culture and to seek better jobs. Moreover, native Anglo-Jews supported immigrants in their efforts to speak English because they disdained Yiddish.

Farjeon also protests against bigotry in England, and he portrays four bigots, covering all classes, to insure his audience's cognizance of difficulties Jews experienced when they had to face and fight anti-Semitism. *Solomon Isaacs* (1877), published twice in 1877, in New York and London, and again in 1883 as *Mrs. Solomon Isaacs,* is a tale of the rise and fall of an old clothes peddler. In this novel· a lower-class bigot resorts to Jew-baiting and fisticuffs. A fight in London's Spitalfields, an East-End area where lower-class immigrants of all nationalities live, illustrates what can occur when racial slurs are vocalized. A shop-owner known as Vampire

raged and stamped in front of his shop, uttering dreadful imprecations, and challenging Solomon Isaacs to come on and have it out like a man. If his allusions had been confined to the object of his wrath, the neighbors would have listened to them with enjoyment and satisfaction; but as they affected the general body of the Hebrew community, it was not long before the Vampire found himself pitted against a score or two of indignant neighbors, whose nerves were quivering at the insults hurled against their religion by the irate Milesian. This suited him exactly; he was in his element; and very soon all Spitalfields was in a ferment. Never was a call to arms more eagerly responded to.[6]

From the foregoing it seems that Vampire's desire to fight impels him to indulge in anti-Semitic "allusions." Whether or not he is an anti-Semite cannot be gauged from this, his only appearance in the novel, but Vampire knows exactly how to rouse his Jewish neighbors and accomplish his need to fight.

Vampire is a lower-class specimen from whom crudeness might be expected. Middle-class bigots in *Aaron the Jew* indulge in anti-Semitism less crudely. With this novel Farjeon created a popular study of the Orthodox Jewish businessman. British editions numbered three between 1894 and 1906; American editions, entitled *A Fair Jewess,* numbered two in the first year of its publication. Two German translations appeared, one during the nineties and one in

1900. The novel allowed Farjeon to illustrate at length the way two anti-Semites try but cannot whip a devout Jew. The admitted anti-Semitic cornchandler and churchwarden, Mr. Whimpole of Gosport, resents Aaron doubly when Aaron refuses to sell Mr. Whimpole the house in which he was born. Because the rest of the community treats Aaron decently, it is safe to assume that it is Whimpole who arranges for neighborhood children to present themselves in front of Aaron's house yelling, "Jew! Jew! Jew!" (116) and for the fire which destroys the house and blinds Aaron's wife. Years later the man still "despises" Aaron (261).

Mr. Poynter, a London contractor, also dislikes Aaron for a dual reason: "He hated Aaron with a very sincere and conscientious hate" (314) because Aaron treated his workmen well and paid them good wages. In addition, Poynter hates Aaron for his Judaism, particularly his benevolence:

He had a bitter hatred of all Jews, and would have willingly subscribed liberally and joined in a crusade to hunt them out of the country. He did not subscribe to the Society for Promoting Christianity among the Jews [sic], because to Christianize them would be to admit them upon terms of equality, and the idea was abhorrent to him. . . . That a Jew could be a good man . . . a just man, or do anything without an eye to profit or self-aggrandisement—these, in his belief, were monstrous propositions . . . certainly no true Christian could entertain them. Mr. Poynter was a Christian, a true Christian, regular in his attendance at church, and fairly liberal, also, in his charities. . . . And here he found another cause for hating Aaron. He heard his name quoted as a man of large benevolence, and he went so far as to declare that Aaron's charities were a means to an end. "He looks upon them as an investment," he said. . . . "Did you ever know a Jew part with his money without an eye to the main chance?" (315)

Poynter maliciously spreads his hatred of Aaron and simultaneously seeks to destroy him: he "fostered a venomous desire to drag Aaron down. . . . He hunted about for the means, he asked questions. It was unquestionably true that there were Jews who had grown rich through dishonesty and usury, and Mr. Poynter did not stop to consider that this applied equally to Christians" (317). Poynter's plot ultimately fails, but his anti-Semitism continues. Without mentioning Aaron's name, he inserts in second-rate journals malicious comments with unmistakeable details that suggest Aaron is a swindler. Failing to disturb Aaron, Poynter attempts to bribe him and again fails. In each exchange Aaron courteously worsts Poynter, but the anti-Semite's bigotry continues to control him. He addresses Aaron sneeringly as a Jew: "Oh, you Jews, you Jews! . . . Always on the look-out for the main chance—always screwing out the last penny" (404). Both Whimpole and Poynter direct their anti-Semitism overtly and covertly toward the object of their hate, avoiding the lower-class Vampire's brawling, and attempt instead insidious methods to ruin a man who refuses to become a victim. These Englishmen's bigotry underscores Aaron's moral behavior, which Farjeon shows is natural to him.

Farjeon's last novel about Jews, *Pride of Race*, was published in England in 1900 and in America in 1901. The novel examines an intermarriage between a wealthy but *nouveau riche* English Jew and an English Protestant. Told from the Christian wife's point of view, it allows the reader to see upper-class anti-Semitism. This union between a Christian woman and a Jewish man is the type cited in historical data about the community as the most frequent, but it and the marriage in Sidgwick's *Lesser's Daughter* are the only Anglo-Jewish novels to depict intermarriage between a Christian woman and a Jewish man. Other Anglo-Jewish novels illustrate intermarriages between a Jewish woman and a Christian man. The Jews and the Christians in *Pride of Race* are Jews and Christians by birth but not by practice, and all but the wife are unreservedly pleased with the match. Raphael Mendoza, whose father acquired his fortune on the stock market, marries Lady Julia Lynwood, whose father inherited a title and poverty. Raphael is happy with Lady Julia, "deeming it natural perhaps that she should hold herself above him, and looking forward to the time when she would sympathise with the aims by which his life was guided."[7] Lady Julia holds herself above Raphael because she believes her father's coercion has doomed her to a loveless marriage with a man both lower in class and a Jew:

Not loveless on her husband's part, but on hers. Devotion more sincere, trust more complete woman never received from man than Lady Julia received from Raphael Mendoza; but, from some warp in her nature which she made no effort to correct, she misconstrued his simplest actions, his simplest words, bringing against him the circumstances of his birth, the class from which he sprung, the religion in which he was born, the wealth his father possessed, and the means by which that wealth had been accumulated. (100)

Moreover, she feels degraded by her marriage: " 'The sight of these people, their sordid scheming, their conversation, the one subject [money] that engrosses them! How low I have fallen, how low, how low!' " (101).

Although Julia's father, the Earl of Lynwood, reminds her that the elder Mendoza saved them from financial ruin, that he was impressed not coerced by Mendoza and Raphael, and most important, that Julia freely chose to marry Raphael, Julia's pride in her ancestry sustains her scorn of the two Jews. She despises Mendoza, who " 'thrust his vulgar personality into every action of our lives' " (108), and Raphael, to whom she believes she was sold. Her coldness to Mendoza and Raphael persists in their company, in the company of others, and in defiance of her father's praise of the Mendozas and his chastisement of her position. Even her conscience reproves her:

Learn from these men whom you have chosen to consider so far beneath you that rank and illustrious descent are valueless when they are not in alliance with worthy deeds, with a life well spent. We live in the present, not in the past, and in the breast of the lowliest man on earth may beat a heart as noble as in that of the prince. Learn the lesson and profit by it—if it be not too late. (286)

Lady Julia disregards her conscience and ungraciously permits Raphael to move out of their home.

She cannot live with Raphael until she learns "through her husband and her husband's father . . . that the world was not made solely for her class, for her race, and that, lacking sympathy with the lowly and the poor, she was less to be considered than the humblest born woman in the land" (338). By the close of the novel, when Lady Julia loses her pride in her ancestry and sees the true merits of Mendoza and Raphael, Farjeon suggests that her marriage has the chance to succeed.

In his studies of anti-Semitism, Farjeon shows the different ways individuals of each class handle bigotry—and the similar nastiness. Fighting and name-calling can be expected from one of the lower class, and name-calling sometimes from the middle class. Farjeon depicts anti-Semites of the middle class as generally preferring insidious, underhanded methods, as do Nina Balatka's relatives when they try to prevent her marriage to a Jew (Trollope, *Nina Balatka*, 1867). People of the upper class in Farjeon's novels are more likely either not to be bigoted—especially when a Jew has money—like the Earl of Lynwood, or privately to despise Jews, like

Lady Julia—even though she marries one. With *Pride of Race* Farjeon
capitalizes on the situation in some English novels, such as in
Trollope's *The Way We Live Now*. Trollope does not allow the
wealthy Jewish girl to marry a titled Englishman. In contrast,
Farjeon permits his wealthy Jew to marry into English nobility and
exposes as well the pain that such a marriage brings. Thackeray
("Rebecca and Rowena") has Rebecca convert, as does Trollope
with his most vulgar Jew, Melmotte; none of Farjeon's characters
even contemplates conversion. Moreover, Farjeon presents one of
the most complete portraits of an intermarriage which occurs during
a nineteenth-century novel, exploiting the situation psychologically,
thematically, and didactically. Reversing the situation of unsympathetic English novels (Trollope may be cited here, too), wherein the
Jew has no choice but to accept Christian scorn or plan revenge,
Farjeon's Jews refuse vengeance. Their fight is either a direct answer
of the moment, as when Solomon Isaacs physically fights Vampire
but harbors no grudge, or a serene faith that their situations will
work out: Aaron refuses to be cowed by extreme ill-treatment,
Raphael Mendoza patiently waits for his wife to mature.

In addition to Farjeon's protest against Jews portrayed as speaking gibberish and against anti-Semitism is his complaint against the
way Jews and Jewish families were depicted by Victorian novelists.
The negative stereotype of the Jewish businessman revealed him to
be craftily waiting or ready to take over the world. Portrayed by
Thackeray in "Codlingsby" (1847), the Jew has already taken over
international business, as the Marquis of Codlingsby reflects, " 'The
Jewish city is lost to Jewish men; but have they not taken the world
in exchange?' "[8] Illustrated at length by Trollope in *The Way We
Live Now* (1876), the Jew, Melmotte, looks "unpleasant and . . .
untrustworthy. . . . [and] as though he were purse-proud and a
bully."[9] Trollope tells the reader that the crude Melmotte is amoral
in his bloated business schemes to make money and wreak revenge:
"People said that Mr. Melmotte had a reputation throughout
Europe as a gigantic swindler,—as one who in the dishonest and
successful pursuit of wealth had stopped at nothing. People said of
him that he had framed and carried out long premeditated and
deeply laid schemes for the ruin of those who had trusted him, that
he had swallowed up the property of all who had come in contact
with him, that he was fed with the blood of widows and children"
(Chapter 8). Although Trollope ascribes these views to rumor, he
shows Melmotte acting precisely as rumor whispers.

Farjeon was no doubt familiar with characterizations like these, if not with these particular unflattering portraits. He attempts to correct prevalent negative beliefs about Jews by linking individual Jews' ethical standards to the practice of Judaism. Whatever his class, a *devout* Jew is never boorish, immoral, or eager to push an Englishman out of his job in Farjeon's novels. Consequently, although Farjeon shows the Jew as unswervingly patriotic to his adopted country whatever his station in life, although he characterizes the Jew as industrious, working his way into a variety of middle-class professions and occupations, and although he illustrates how, as a self-made man, a Jew can be brilliant, charming, and occasionally even capable of disarming an anti-Semite, Farjeon's financiers, philanthropists, writers, and businessmen are flatteringly portrayed only if they are *devout* Jews. Nominal Jews, those who are Jews in name only, whatever their occupations and class, are allowed to be boors, social climbers, and vicious cutthroats.

Farjeon paints such a picture of a nominal Jew in *Solomon Isaacs*. Isaacs is an old clothes peddler who appears to be religious. He attends Sabbath services but has no real knowledge of Judaism, for he "went to synagogue regularly every Sabbath, and mumbled through a form of prayers, of the meaning of which he had as much knowledge as the Man in the Moon" (904). Instead of worshipping God, Isaacs worships money: " 'What do people bow down to?' " he asks, " 'Money. What do people worship? Money. What was the temple made of? Money. What'll buy fine 'ouses, fine clothes, fine diamonds? Money-money-money! There's nothing like money' " (904). To make more, Isaacs speculates "with fear and trembling" on the Stock Exchange (904). Successful there, he begins to lend money and amasses a fortune through both kinds of investments. As a wealthy man, Isaacs promptly sells his old clothes bag, buys vulgar new clothes for himself and his wife, snubs his old friends, compels his poor future daughter-in-law to break her engagement, buys a new house and equips it with gaudy furniture and servants (before whom he is abashed), and anglicizes his name. Isaacs is neither evil nor revenge-ridden as Melmotte is. Isaacs does not enjoy the process of making money like Melmotte does but, like Melmotte, grows addicted to it. Moreover, his unsuccessful attempts to become respectable sadden his family and friends, who cannot persuade him away from his endeavors. In addition, because Isaacs does not truly adhere to Judaism, he treats his wife poorly. Mrs. Isaacs accepts her husband's word as law. Although she dislikes the social climbing he requires of her, she shows her unhappiness only when she is alone, revealing more self-pride than Mrs. Melmotte. Apparently having as little sympathy for the nominal Jew as Trollope had for unavowed Jews, Farjeon resolves the plot by punishing Isaacs. He "awoke one morning to find himself more famous than ever. . . . He . . . found himself torn and bleeding—a laughing stock . . . a ruined man and a beggar" (913). Unlike Trollope, to whom all Jews were upstarts, vulgarians, and social invaders, Farjeon makes a distinction between nominal and devout Jews. The nominal Jew can be as vulgar and cruel as Trollope portrays him. For Farjeon, living in accord with Jewish ethics—which Isaacs plainly fails to do—makes the difference.

Farjeon's earliest Jewish businessman is an incidental character in *At the Sign of the Silver Flagon*, which appeared the same year *The Way We Live Now* was published in book form. With his Jewish salesman, Mr. Nathan, Farjeon illustrates how the devout Jew is a very different man. A bachelor, Mr. Nathan owns a men's haberdashery and exudes the magnetism of the successful salesman, "being, as are all of his race, singularly tenacious in the negotiation of a bargain. . . . He would make you buy a thing if you did not want it. That you did not want it did not matter to him; he had it to sell. To sell was his business; and in his business he, as a representative man, beat the world" (62). In bargaining, Nathan attempts to disguise his kindliness, but his actions reveal it, as when he makes terms for his lodgers: " 'I'll make them suit you,' said Mr. Nathan, with a strange obliviousness of self-interest" (62). Although Nathan is eager to make a deal, he is not a greedy man.

Unlike Solomon Isaacs and Melmotte, Nathan boasts of his Judaism saying, " 'I *am* a Jew, and I'm proud of it, proud of it' " (62). In addition, Nathan lives in accord with Jewish teachings insofar as he will neither marry a Christian woman because "their religions were different" nor convert (93). Nathan lives as a devout Jew and thus is able to withstand worldly temptations. Further overturning the negative stereotype of men like Melmotte and his equally rapacious henchman, Cohenlupe, Farjeon capitalizes on Nathan's appearance: "He was loosely and somewhat slovenly dressed, but his eye was so wonderfully sparkling, and his handsome face . . . wore such a cheerful and almost philanthropic expression, that the chances were if your eyes rested once upon him you would turn to look again" (61–62). Farjeon thus indicates that not all Jews are fat, greasy, and untrustworthy. Nathan is "somewhat slovenly dressed," but he acts courteously, like other Englishmen. Moreover, he believes, " 'You wouldn't take me for a Jew from my appearance' " (62). Farjeon's ironic commentary on Nathan's belief, that this was "a strange hallucination indulged in by many of the race, for the speaker's Jewish cast of features was unmistakeable" (62), reveals the thrust of his characterization: Jews may be tenacious salesmen, but not all Jews are evil nor are they looking out only for themselves. Indeed, by giving Nathan two attributes some Englishmen believed all Jews possessed—slovenly dress and Jewish features—Farjeon indulges those readers and then undercuts the major components of the stereotype—rapacity and exploitation—which, he shows, do not necessarily belong to careless dress and Jewish features. Farjeon's use of an incidental character in *Silver Flagon* permits him genially to correct English views.

With *Silver Flagon* Farjeon begins to counter the negative English stereotype of the Jewish businessman. With Aaron Cohen (*Aaron the Jew*) and Moses Mendoza (*Pride of Race*), Farjeon completes his task. Like Mr. Nathan, Aaron Cohen and Moses Mendoza take pride in their Judaism (although each differs in the way he expresses his belief); they are consistently honest in their business dealings and show genuine love for their families. Published in 1894, *Aaron the Jew* examines the rise and fall of an Orthodox Jewish building contractor. Aaron's creed, "that it is man's duty to do right, to work, to pray, to be considerate to his neighbors, to make his home cheerful, to be as charitable as his means will allow" (134), is assuredly a rather tepid statement of Judaism. Nonetheless, he adheres to this philosophy from the time he is a poor pawnbroker through his days as a wealthy contractor who pays his workmen good wages, trusting "in God—yes; but he knew that a man must work for his livelihood" (153). As a wealthy, charitable man, Aaron continues to make "prayer . . . part of his life" (155). "Hailed as a worthy upholder of the old faith" (252), Aaron remains "against the backsliding of the modern Jew who was disposed to adapt his life to the altered circumstances of the times" (323); and he often encourages others to be proud they are Jews. Because his life bears strict public scrutiny, business reverses and cruel rumors fail to affect him and his family. Most important, his adherence to Judaism permits Aaron cheerfully to live with less money when, at the end of the novel, his business has been ruined by an anti-Semite. Reversing Trollope's scenario which leaves Melmotte ruined and with no alternative other than suicide, Farjeon illustrates how a Jew can fail in business yet accept his lot—and Aaron can because he is devout.

Aaron differs from Melmotte and other negative English stereotypes, too, in the way he treats his family. The stereotype shows the Jew concerned about his money foremost and his child, usually a daughter, only second. He generally has no wife; when he does, like Melmotte, he treats her cruelly, beating and making fun of her. To counter negative depictions of the Jew as family head, Farjeon portrays Aaron as always having time for his wife and daughter, despite his business pressures. A considerate, loving husband and father, Aaron treats his wife like a child. In proper Victorian fashion, he blesses her in one instance as a father would his daughter and protects her from important decisions throughout their married life on the premise that sharing decisions would give her pain and disturb her faith in him. With the characterizations of Aaron and Ruth Cohen, Farjeon competently answers Trollope and other novelists who negatively stereotyped Jews.

In *Pride of Race* Farjeon depicts another honest Jewish businessman. Shrewd Moses Mendoza also rises from a "common sordid calling" (43) to a "millionaire Stock Exchange speculator" (51). He, too, is proud to be a Jew, but his Judaism expresses itself through love for his son and charity for all rather than in prayer. He neglects Orthodox dietary laws saying, "We're not particular as we used to be. Times are changed" (16). "An uneducated, ignorant man, his common breeding stamped on his good-humoured features, and expressing itself in his gutteral voice" (29), Mendoza wants his son, Raphael, to have the education he never had: " 'I want 'im to go away from me, right away from me and the people I mix with; I want 'im to be in a place where he can mix with gentlemen, and learn' " (14−15).

This desire to educate Raphael, in accord with Jewish precept, is not fulfilled without Mendoza's self-sacrifice: "It was to the end of giving Raphael the best education that could be obtained that he had saved and pared and pinched, denying himself every indulgence that would make the least demand upon his purse" (23). When Raphael attends an excellent school, Mendoza "did not present himself again at the school. . . . He would not humiliate his son by the intrusion of his personality" (37). Discovering that he is a born financier, Mendoza instinctively wishes to make money, but not for himself: "Naturally he wished to make money, but chiefly for Raphael's sake" (45). Mendoza treats his son in a far different manner from Melmotte who treats his daughter as property to be disposed of at his will. Unlike Marie Melmotte, Raphael reciprocates his father's love. When Mendoza suffers business reverses

Raphael gives up his seat in Parliament and pays his father's creditors, displaying exemplary behavior and love comparable to his father's for him. At the end of the novel Mendoza and Raphael resume, like Aaron, a less comfortable life but one rich with family love.

Aaron and Mendoza differ mainly in their practice of Judaism. Both make and lose fortunes but remain loving family men, consistently honest in their dealings with others. Aaron and Mendoza live their religion. Aaron makes occasions for prayer a part of his life; Mendoza, through his example, raises his son to be an honest man. The inescapable conclusion to be drawn from the examples of Aaron and Mendoza is that Judaism can and should form the ethic on which to build the practice of business and of life; this conclusion can only be reinforced by the example of Solomon Isaacs who appears to be a devout Jew but whose business practice and worship of money indicate two separate ethics and belie projected appearances.

To the legacy of unflattering and often cruel stereotypes, Farjeon answers with three idealized Jewish characters. His effectiveness lies in his knowledge and use of Judaism. Farjeon makes clear that the negative English stereotype rests on the frequent bloating of a few attributes entrenched in characterizations of all Jews. A comparison with his own characters demonstrates that the creators of the negative stereotype generally ignore Judaism as a practiced religion, preferring to embody in their Jews revenge as a Jewish tenet. Charles Reade, for example, shows Isaac Levi (*It Is Never Too Late to Mend*) as following the supposed Jewish concept of "an eye for an eye"; thus Levi seeks revenge. The correct English translation of the Hebrew is "an eye *under* an eye," which means *fair*, not exact, compensation (Exodus 21:24; Leviticus 24:19). Jews are commanded to pursue not revenge but justice and peace (Numbers 16:22; Isaiah 2:3−4). Through Nathan, Cohen, and Mendoza, despite the sentimentality of their characterizations, Farjeon illustrates the devout Jew. Taken together with the nominal Jew, Soloman Isaacs, Farjeon's portrayals indicate that one cannot carelessly append a derogatory name to all he or she assumes to be evil. One must know for what a person stands and in what that person believes. Only then can one judge and speak, as Farjeon clearly does in refuting the negative stereotype of the Jew.

CHAPTER 5

The Challenge from Within: Assimilation and Intermarriage

THE third challenge to which Anglo-Jewish novelists responded came not from anti-Semitism or from Christian attempts to convert Jews. It came from within the Anglo-Jewish community itself as Jews tried to answer the question of how to be simultaneously a good Jew and a good Victorian. The novelists responded to this challenge as well as to problems closely associated with it—assimilation, intermarriage, and immigration. This last challenge appears to have been irresolvable in any single definitive manner.

During the last two decades of Victoria's reign particularly, Anglo-Jews generally took one of three routes in an effort to achieve balance. One avenue frequently taken was to remain Orthodox and separate from English society. Many other Anglo-Jews modified their practice of Judaism as Meritor had anticipated in 1857, but although they did not entirely separate themselves from other Victorians, they remained essentially Jewish. A third dominant path was total assimilation, either through intermarriage or the renunciation of Judaism. Thus some Jews disappeared into English society and were lost to the Jewish community. Whether native or immigrant, each individual had to resolve how much Judaism to retain.

Later Anglo-Jewish novelists responded to this problem of assimilation. Although the community tolerated acculturation to a degree, many individuals, some novelists included, looked askance on assimilation and intermarriage. They recognized that Jews who assimilated or intermarried, even in instances in which they did not formally become Christians, in essence had left the community. Indeed, two novelists, Amy Levy and Julia Frankau, show acculturation bordering on assimilation and thereby permitting the rise of the

despised materialistic Jew Trollope had caricatured during the
1870s. While Emily Marian Harris observes the different ways Jews
face pressures of assimilation and intermarriage without judgment,
Amy Levy and Julia Frankau view severely the Jew who modifies his
or her religion in order to worship the Golden Calf.

I   *Emily Marian Harris*

Emily Marian Harris (1844—1900) wrote at least one volume of
poetry, an essay, and twelve novels, two of which examine Anglo-
Jews who feel feel the pressures of assimilation and intermarriage.
Each of these novels went through only one edition. Harris's seventh
novel is her first about Jews. *Estelle* (1878) tells the story of a Jewish
family, the Hofers, who live in a small English cathedral town.
Totally isolated from fellow Jews, they manage nonetheless to raise
their daughters, Lexie and Estelle, to young womanhood as Orthodox Jews.[1] The bulk of Harris's sympathetic narrative plumbs the
complications the Hofer sisters discover as they try to establish
friendships with the Christian Haye sisters. Although their father,
the scholarly strict Dr. Hofer, suspects the Christian women of
being interested in his daughters only to satisfy their curiosity about
Jewish habits and their religion, he wisely permits his daughters to
see the Haye sisters because he realizes that to forbid them would be
to stimulate further their curiosity. He relies on his daughters'
Jewish upbringing to keep them from harm.

Hofer's suspicions about the Haye sisters prove true, for the
young Christian women delight in Lexie and Estelle's company
until they recognize their brother Cecil's and a cousin's partiality
for the Jewish sisters. Although the Haye sisters taunt Lexie and
Estelle to prevent intermarriage, it is the Hofer sisters' Jewish
upbringing rather than these taunts that decides the issue. Lexie
chooses to marry a Jewish man; Estelle determines to remain single
instead of marrying the Christian Cecil Haye. In *Estelle* both
Christians and Jews disapprove of intermarriage, although individuals of each religion perceive the "problem" of Judaism in a different
way.

In this quiet, dignified but often humorous novel, Estelle exercises
a strong influence on the Christian men of her acquaintance. She
sets the example for conformity to one's religion, particularly in the
areas of intermarriage and charity. Estelle's deep religious conviction and her freely chosen self-denial cause Cecil and a few of his

family to alter their preconceived ideas of Judaism, Jews, and their supposed monetary wealth. Her later visits to poor Jews cause another Christian man to begin working with the poor of his own religion.

Benedictus (1887) continues the story of Estelle's single life in London and concentrates on the Jewish friends, mostly Russian-Polish immigrants, she makes there.[2] In this novel Harris contrasts Estelle and her poorer friends with wealthy accultured English-born Jews and with Benedictus, the alienated Roumanian Jew. Estelle and her poorer friends cling to Jewish rituals as well as to the tradition of educating Jewish children, whereas her wealthy Anglo-Jewish friends no longer adhere to Orthodox Judaism. They celebrate only the major festivals and one of this group intermarries, but they all continue to live the Jewish commandment to be charitable. Like Estelle, they teach poor Jews. Acculturation, Harris indicates, makes some Jews chafe against traditional restrictions but does not necessarily detach Jews from religious ethics.

In the case of Benedictus, the reader views a more complex set of circumstances for abandoning Judaism. Raised as an Orthodox Jew, Benedictus separates himself from Jewish law and Jewish institutions. He does so because his persecuted Roumanian brethren refuse to help themselves even after he donates his inheritance to aid them. Benedictus concludes that they are hopelessly fettered by Orthodoxy; consequently, he forsakes them and Judaism. Arriving in England, Benedictus wants to end the persecutions of Jews, but he does not act. As a practicing Jew, Benedictus was an energetic, active man; now, he drifts through life, forming no attachments. The implicit comparison between Benedictus the practicing Jew and Benedictus the alienated Jew suggests, as in the case of Farjeon's Solomon Isaacs, and as we shall see, Julia Frankau's Dr. Phillips, that a Jew performs little effective moral work without religious conviction.

In her two novels Harris shows how Jews react differently to the pressures of assimilation and intermarriage. Some yield their Orthodoxy, one intermarries, Benedictus drifts away from Jews and out of the novel, but the newer immigrants and Estelle remain steadfast Jews. Harris depicts the problems late nineteenth-century Jews face and the ways they solve their dilemmas. She indicates that Jews are individuals, like Christians, and meet difficulties not always according to religious precept but often according to individual inclination. Moreover, Harris condoles with her characters; she allows each his or her final choice without narrative judgment. Harris suggests that the ways of the late Victorian world are problematic; each Jew must find his or her own path in that world and individually define a relation to Judaism.

II   *Amy Levy*

Amy Levy (1861–1889) was a poet, essayist, translator, short-story writer, and novelist. The first Jewish girl to matriculate at Newnham College, Cambridge, Levy began publishing as an undergraduate in 1880. She was a close friend of Constance and Richard Garnett and Olive Schreiner, an English novelist with Jewish blood but not a practicing Jew. Before she committed suicide, Levy's publications included four volumes of poetry, two novels, articles on Jewish humor, Jewish children, Jewish ghettoes in Italy, and the Jew in fiction, as well as various short stories. One short story and one novel deal with Jews.[3] In the short story, "Cohen of Trinity," published a few months before she died, Levy depicts a Jew, Cohen, who publishes a brilliant book. Realizing that his literary success will not bring him the recognition for which he secretly yearns, Cohen commits suicide. Levy's non-Jewish narrator indicates that Cohen's wish for recognition, "a desire to stand well in another's eyes," is a Jewish trait, "a marked characteristic of the Jewish people."[4] It is not known whether Levy committed suicide for the same reason—her novel about Jews had met with an unfavorable reaction—but the story does detail a Jew's despair at not finding the exact success of which he dreamed.

While Levy deplores in her essays the fact that English fiction, even *Daniel Deronda*, presents " 'no serious treatment of Jewish life and Jewish character nor any true picture of contemporary Anglo-Jewish life,' " she is very much concerned that many Jews seem " 'undisturbed by inherited racial memory.' "[5] Levy complains that the old Jewish traditions are disappearing, that Jewish parents spoil their children, and that perhaps only Jewish humor preserves family feeling among Jews (Abrahams, 14). Jews untroubled by racial memory or true belief are the subject of her novel, *Reuben Sachs; A Sketch* (1888). *Reuben Sachs* met with Anglo-Jewish displeasure, yet the novel went through three editions, the last of which appeared in 1945. In *Reuben Sachs*, Levy maliciously depicts the Anglo-Jewish community. In addition to portraying late nineteenth-century accultured middle-class Jews as gradually yielding to the pressures of assimilation and intermarriage, as grappling unsuccessfully with the issues of conversion and the philosophy by which one should live, Levy shows them to be snobbish materialists. Conjointly, she negatively links her depictions of these Jews to all.

The Sachs-Leuniger clan of Jews in *Reuben Sachs* have accultured but they have not yet assimilated. They are not religiously observant Jews; they vie with each other for the possession of the highest caste of Jewish and non-Jewish friends, and they are proud to have non-Jewish acquaintances. Moreover, while they frown on intermarriage, they are tolerant about conversion. Like Gordon, Levy opposes conversion to Judaism because she feels that Jews must remain Jews and that Jewish hopes for a durable marriage depend upon the espousal of a coreligionist. Like Gordon, Levy examines what the convert feels and does about Judaism once he is called a Jew. Unlike Gordon, Levy presents the convert as a hypocrite and the Jewish community as realizing but failing to act on his duplicity because their interest lies in money.

To bring into relief the convert's duplicity and the community's hypocrisy, Levy establishes that the community has the facts but does not use them. One member of the Sachs-Leuniger clan remarks about the convert, Bertie Lee-Harrison, " 'He would more likely be considered a fool for his pains [to convert].' "[6] Another had met him at Pontresina when he was a High Churchman "and hardly knew a Jew from a Mohammedan" (57). The younger members of the family are more impressed with his family connections than with his conversion. In addition, the well-to-do Bertie emerges not as a man searching for spiritual peace but as a dilettante alternating between earnest involvement in his new religion and sociological investigation. Bertie's demeanor attests to the fact that sociological investigation, not the search for spiritual peace, dominates him: Bertie "bear[s] on his amiable, commonplace, neatly modelled little face no traces of the spiritual conflict which anyone knowing his history might have supposed him to have passed through" (83). Bertie comes to Judaism with a history of switching religions:

"He says himself . . . he has a taste for religion. . . . He flirted with the Holy Mother for some years, but didn't get caught. Then he joined a set of mystics, and lived for three months on a mountain, somewhere in Asia Minor. Now he has come round to thinking Judaism the one religion, and has been regularly received into the synagogue." (24)

According to the protagonist, Reuben Sachs, Bertie searches less for the "one religion" than for "local colour": " 'He has a seat in Berkeley Street [the Reform synagogue], and a brand new *talith*, but still he is not happy. He complains that the Jews he meets in society are unsatisfactory; they have not local colour' "(25). Reuben's belief that Bertie searches more for "local colour" is borne out by the convert's behavior and comments, but the community fails to concern itself with the truth.

Whenever the narrative impinges on Judaism, Bertie reveals himself as a person involved with Judaism only superficially. Because his attention remains concentrated on Jews rather than on Judaism, Bertie can neither involve himself with his new religion nor develop a sense of kinship with his new coreligionists. Thus, he goes "through the day's proceedings [on the Day of Atonement] with all the zeal of a convert" (93), but his remarks in synagogue are restricted to the observation "that the Jewish ladies were certainly very lovely" (89). Coming to break the Day of Atonement fast with Reuben's clan, Bertie acts like an ebullient adolescent. Bertie, "who had come in with Reuben, pale, exhausted, but prepared to be impressed by every thing and every one he saw, confided to his friend that the twenty-four hours' fast had been the severest ordeal he had as yet undergone in the service of religion—his experiences in Asia Minor not excepted" (95). Bertie may be prepared to be impressed, but he is bewildered by what ensues because he possesses no sense of kinship with Jews: "Bertie stared and Bertie wondered. Needless to state, he was completely out of touch with these people whose faith his search for the true religion had led him, for the time being, to embrace" (110). The pervasive feeling that Bertie converted to Judaism for "local colour" also undermines the seriousness with which he participates in the observance of the High Holy Days and Succot. Moreover, he tells Reuben after they break the fast, " 'I am deeply interested in the Jewish character . . . the strongly marked contrasts; the underlying resemblances; the elaborate differentiations from a fundamental type!' " (111). Both Bertie's comments and those of the narrator reinforce the fact that Bertie's urge to convert has been one to investigate rather than to find peace. Very possibly Bertie's failure to develop a sense of kinship with Jews, and so identify with Judaism at least culturally, may be another way through which Levy indicates her opposition to conversion.

Bertie's interest in Jews grows into a marriage proposal to the Sephardic Judith Quixano. At this juncture the older Jews appraise Bertie more carefully. Judith's mother, deeply upset, hesitates because she realizes Bertie's Judaism is, despite outward appearances, a momentary involvement. Her brother, Israel Leuniger, and his wife attempt "to convince her that Bertie's spurious Judaism could . . . be accepted as the real thing": " 'My dear Golda, he is as much a Jew as you or I. Her father is perfectly satisfied, as well he may be—it is a brilliant match' "(222). Because "Mrs. Leuniger realized perfectly the meaning of £5,000 a year" (223), she counsels Judith's mother to accept the marriage; accordingly, from being "not pleased at heart," Mrs. Quixano finally becomes "very anxious for the marriage" (227). The novel disapproves of the union, but once the family accepts Bertie, the Jewish community accepts the match because he has formally become a Jew. Levy thus shows Anglo-Jews to be so interested in money that they ignore the fact of Bertie's spurious Judaism.

Despite its acceptance of Bertie the community criticizes Judith, for it feels she should have married a born Jew: "The Community, after much discussion, much shaking of heads over the degeneracy of the times, had decided on accepting Bertie's veneer of Judaism as the real thing, and the engagement was treated like any other"; however, "the brilliancy of the match was considered a little dimmed by the fact of Bertie's not being of the Semitic race. It showed indifferent sportsmanship [on Judith's part], if nothing else, to have failed in bringing down one of the wily sons of Shem" (234-35). Antithetical to the community's tolerance, some of Judith's Orthodox relatives insist that it is a mixed marriage anyway. Bertie's family basically shares their opinion. Although they like Judith, they find her family "uncongenial, if not worse" (250).

Levy contrasts all these attitudes to Bertie's, showing his public practice of Judaism at his wedding to be far different from the way he will later live. With religious zeal equal to that he had displayed during the Jewish holidays, he enjoys his wedding "immensely, going through the whole pageant with great exactness, smashing the wine-glass vigorously with his little foot, and sipping the wine daintily from the silver cup" (248−49). When the novel ends three months after his wedding, Bertie has abandoned Judaism, however, and his bride, Judith, has been severed from her people, so that she experiences "an inrushing sense of exile" with no real hope of return: "Her people—oh, her people!—to be back once more among them. When all was said, she had been so happy there" (258). Through her negative view of the convert to Judaism, Levy shows the convert's hypocrisy, the community's willingness to ignore it, and Judith's actual—if neither voluntary nor intentional—assimilation. That Bertie fails to become truly Jewish despite the known rigors of conversion to Judaism does not imply that Levy is ignorant of or ignores these difficulties. Rather, her documenting his history of passing through other religious rigors tranquilly and spiritually unmoved confirms that she intends the reader to judge Bertie harshly. In *Reuben Sachs* Levy thus indicts not only the dilettante convert but also the hypocritical Jew who knows the convert's Judaism to be spurious but who accepts him anyway.

A second way Levy indicates her thorough disapproval of accultured middle-class Jews is by emphasizing their materialism, which she argues is leavened with an obsession for social status. The elder members of the Sachs-Leuniger clan instill into their children the desire for material success in all forms. In particular, old Solomon Sachs, the patriarch, seems to have engendered in them this philosophy, for he "had been a hard man in his dealings with the world; never overstepping the line of legal honesty, but taking an advantage wherever he could do so with impunity" (52). Only when too aged to work does he return to saying prayers, "an occupation which helped him to get rid of a great deal of his time, which hung heavily on his hands, now that age had disabled him from active service on the Stock Exchange" (46—47).

From this background the two major characters emerge as self-serving. Reuben eschews his love for his cousin, Judith Quixano, in order to advance his political ambitions; overthrown, Judith marries Bertie Lee-Harrison, the "boring" convert, to reach the summit of the "social heights" before Reuben (227). Reuben rationalizes himself out of marrying Judith by remembering that

from his cradle he had imbibed the creed that it is noble and desirable to have everything better than your neighbor; from the first had been imposed on him the sacred duty of doing the very best for yourself.

Yes, he was in love; cruelly, inconveniently, most unfortunately in love. But ten years hence, when he would still be a young man, the fever would certainly have abated, would be a dream of the past, while his ambition he had no doubt would be as lusty as ever. (126)

Judith's upbringing has been equally oriented toward material relationships:

The practical, if not the theoretical, teaching of her life had been to treat as absurd any close or strong feeling which had not its foundation in material interests. There must be no undue giving away of one's self in friendship, in the pursuit of ideas, in charity, in a public cause. (201–202)

Instead, "material advantage; things that you could touch and see and talk about; that these were the only things which really mattered had been the unspoken gospel of her life" (232–33). Believing this, Judith comprehends Reuben's unspoken point of view, accepting that, "if this doctrine applied to friendship, to philanthropy, to art and politics, [then] in how much greater a degree must it apply to love" (202). It is according to the materialistic philosophy of "taking the best that you could get for yourself" (233) that Judith accepts Bertie Lee-Harrison. Levy punishes these two young people for wearing blinders to what is truly important. Reuben fulfills his ambition to win an election but dies before he learns the news; Judith marries Bertie and is cut off from everyone she knows.

Levy indicates, moreover, that the desire for material and social success produces base hypocrisy. Members of the Sachs-Leuniger clan keep up only the appearance of being Jewish and rationalize their actions. Israel Leuniger rose from clerk to partner in a brokerage firm and married a partner's daughter. A "thorough-going pagan," he no longer practices Judaism, yet he

would have set his foot mercilessly on such an arrangement [as intermarriage]; it would not have seemed to him respectable. He was no stickler for forms and ceremonies; though while old Solomon lived a certain amount of observances of them was necessary; you need only marry a Jew and be buried at Willesden or Ball's Pond [Jewish cemeteries]; the rest would take care of itself. (36)

Consequently, Leuniger can evade the question of Bertie Lee-Harrison's Jewishness and want the marriage for Judith's material and social advantage. Leuniger's son, Leo, also illustrates the urge for social success with a hypocrite's élan. He "affected to despise class distinctions, but succeeded in getting himself invited to . . . 'good' houses" (57).

Through the various members of the clan, Levy argues that Jews who pursue material success easily subordinate all morally important matters to pride, social advancement, and gossip—trivia. Montague Cohen is proud of his masculinity "to an even greater extent than most men of his race" (49). "Led by the nose by his wife," however, Cohen passes "his life in pursuit of a shadow which is called social advancement" (49). His wife, Adelaide, with her "dancing, glittering, hard little organs of vision," possesses "to the full, the gregarious instincts of her race, and Whiteley's [a department store] was her happy hunting ground. Here, on this neutral territory . . . could her boundless curiosity be gratified, here could her love of gossip have free play" (71).

Furthermore, they are cruel. Levy exposes these Jews' cruelty, born of smugness at how far they have risen, when she shows them laughing at their poor cousins, the Samuel Sachses, for their Orthodoxy:

Their appearance, gestures, their excruciating method of pronouncing the English language, the hundred and one tribal peculiarities which clung to them, had long served their cousins as a favourite family joke. . . . They were indeed, as Reuben had said, a remarkable survival. (102)

Although Levy suggests that the wealthier Jews snub the Sachses because of their Orthodoxy, she also sees that the Sachses' poverty demeans their cousins, as when she comments, "The Jewish people, so eager to crown success in any form, so determined in laying claim to the successful among their number, have scant love for those unfortunates who have dropped behind in the race" (107).

Levy's disgust at these Jews and others like them emerges clearly. Common to these by no means exhaustive examples of how family members achieve visible success, whether it be to appear religious, democratic, the man of the family, or to share a joke at someone's expense, is the narrative link between the trait and the religion, a major way in which Levy underscores her hostility. Accompanying her deprecating characterizations are generalizations about all Jews. Thus, she says Reuben's "good clothes" cannot "disguise the fact that his figure was bad, and his movements awkward; unmistakeably the figure and movements of a Jew" (11), while "Leo was by no means free from the tribal foible of inquisitiveness" (130). All Jewish males share Montague Cohen's pride of sex in the morning prayer: " 'Blessed art Thou, O Lord my God who hast not made me a woman.' No prayer goes up from the synagogue with greater fervour than this" (49). A party affords an opportunity for the inclusion of gratuitous narrative sniping at Jews:

If there is strong family feeling among the children of Israel, it takes often the form of acute family jealousy. The Jew who will open his doors in reckless ignorance to every sort and condition of Gentile is morbidly sensitive as regards the social standing of the compatriot whom he admits to his hospitality. (146—47)

While the foregoing comment restricts itself to some Jews, the following encompasses all: "The charms of person which a Jew or Jewess may possess are not usually such as will bear the test of being regarded as a whole. Some quite commonplace English girls and men . . . looked positively beautiful as they moved about among the ill-made sons and daughters of Shem" (152).

In *Reuben Sachs* not only does the individual Jew's propulsion toward success and material advantage come under fire, but all Jews are disapproved of for having false pride in their masculinity; for being inferior in figure, movements as well as pettily competitive; and for pretending to be superior to their own people. The materialistic, success-oriented Jew caricatured thirteen years earlier by Trollope in *The Way We Live Now* accumulates particularly invidious traits here. Levy probably wanted to correct negative tendencies; in fact she describes Jews who come to a bad end because of their materialistic philosophy; suggests that all Jews are like this clan; and generalizes about all Jews in the same manner as some English novelists—all of which concepts may go beyond her intention.

Perhaps Levy expected her delineation of accultured Jews who yield to the pressures of assimiliation to effect positive changes in the community because the criticism in *Reuben Sachs* emanated from a Jew, for her narrator acknowledges that "the Jews, the most clannish and exclusive of peoples, the most keen to resent outside criticism, can say hard things of one another within the walls of the ghetto" (24). But with this novel's publication Levy's criticisms moved out of the ghetto into the public domain and were regarded by the community just as portrayals by English novelists were. Indeed, Levy's firsthand knowledge of the materialistic Jew may have disgusted her far more than it did the English and so impelled her to write. Her linkage of all Jews to this type through her generalizations, however, implies a bigotry equal to that of some English novelists.

III *Julia Frankau*

A sister of James Davis—a journalist, dramatist, and composer of comic operas who wrote under the name of Owen Hall—Julia Frankau (1859—1916) was an art critic, short-story writer, parodist, and novelist. Her family, all writers, lost their contact with Judaism. Mrs. Paul Lafargue, a daughter of Karl Marx (himself baptized at the age of six), raised Frankau. Frankau's son, Gilbert, became a novelist, and her granddaughter, Pamela, also a novelist, converted to Catholicism. Frankau published her fifteen novels, four of which deal with Jews, under the name of Frank Danby.[7] As might be expected from one exposed to Marx's views, Frankau concerns herself with Jewish materialism. Her negative feelings about various types of Jews encompass a breadth Levy's novel does not. Frankau's antipathy for money-grubbing Jews appears primarily in *Dr. Phillips; A Maida Vale Idyll* (1887). Her other novels examine the immigrant; these are discussed in Chapter 6. In all four novels Frankau denigrates Jews.

Frankau's earliest novel is also her first to deal with materialism in the Jewish community. Although one bibliographer says it was suppressed in England and America because of its "realistic treatment" of wealthy middle-class Jews, *Dr. Phillips* went through five English editions in ten years and was issued twice in America.[8] In the preface to the second edition to appear in 1887, Frankau protests that her novel is not an attack on all Jews but on a "small and little known section of society before it yields to the influences of advanced civilization and education. For personal reasons I regret that this small section owns Judaism as a religion."[9] Like Levy's community, Frankau's materialistic opportunists are Orthodox Jews, but they are not hypocrites—they openly pursue what they want.

In *Dr. Phillips* no Jew thwarts love from a desire for money or status as he or she does in *Reuben Sachs*, but the desire for money and social advantage compels Frankau's characters as much as the naked urge for material success controls Levy's. Like Levy, Frankau generalizes about Jews, but her comments arise organically. Thus, while they project an attitude as snide and as varied as Levy's, they are not gratuitous. All of them arise from Frankau's belief that the Jews' God is Gain: "The great single Deity, the 'I am the Lord thy God, and thou shalt have no other,' that binds Judaism together, is as invincible now as it was when Moses had to destroy the Golden Calf on Mount Horeb. And that Deity is Gain" (15).

Worship at the shrine of money dominates the major Jewish characters in the novel. It transforms Dr. Phillips, the protagonist, for whom money and social advantage become inextricably entwined. Because Phillips is the most complex character in this body of novels—Frankau links his materialism to his nature and his vocation—I examine him at length. A Jewish materialist with a sensuous nature, Phillips married "when, and because, his fortunes were at a very low ebb. His wife had interposed between him and ruin; and with the dowry she had brought him he had purchased a practice in Portsdown Road, Maida Vale, and commenced his career of popularity" (27). A "ladies' doctor" (16), Phillips looks "upon women as subordinate beings, made but for one purpose, born with but one mission" (238). Consequently, he despises his wife but derives comfort from their relationship: "Poisonous as was the influence she undoubtedly had over him, a certain sensuous pleasure that woman's society had for him linked her to him in a bond that, if not one of affection, was curiously like it" (38). Phillips's feelings for his wife, his love of money, and his enjoyment of female society change his medical practice. He becomes indolent and greedy and takes a non-Jewish mistress:

His character retrograded. . . . Women liked him naturally, and his adaptable nature enabled him to secure and utilize that liking. He made money, bought a carriage for his wife, and Mrs. Cameron for himself. The man of whom his colleagues at the hospital had predicted such great things, the man who had so easily taken prize after prize contended for by hundreds of his contemporaries, the man who, according to his tutors and his lecturers, was to be the greatest surgeon of his time, the man whose delicate touch at the operation table had been the admiration of the whole theatre, had degenerated into the pet of Maida Vale drawing rooms. (28)

The practice of medicine for money prevents Phillips from rising above his own sensuous nature:

His powers and intellect failed. . . . All these women, his wife, his patients, and others, clung around him, and were gradually killing his heart and mind and conscience. He had too much to struggle against, and the physical comforts of his home, added to his indolence and Jewish love of comfort, dragged him helplessly down in the octopus arms of many tempters. (28 – 29)

Nonetheless, Phillips retains his medical skill. He has the "gift of diagnosis. . . . He could read life or death on a patient's face with unerring instinct" (71), and his professional brethren enjoy consulting him.

After a while Phillips's indolence, created by wealth, encourages his sensuosity and dangerously affects his practice:

Once Brain had been his God, and his passions trivial incidents. He had started in his profession with ardour, he had studied with avidity the secrets of life and death, and had held them sacred. But the luxurious prostitution of his marriage had developed in him an Eastern virility that brooked no denial.

His nature craved excitement; he had never found it with his wife, he no longer found it in a struggle with his competitors. He commenced to play with his knowledge. He experimentalized, half idly, half maliciously; the lives that were at that time in his keeping had trembled in the balance, and had been sacrificed to a curiosity which was not a thirst for knowledge. (94–95)

Phillips shares important qualities with George Eliot's physician, Lydgate (*Middlemarch*, 1872). Both men are fascinated with reason and science, and both are dragged down by their sensuous natures. But there the similarity ends; Lydgate does not experiment with his patients nor does he take a mistress. Phillips credits his Christian mistress with saving him from gambling with humanity. In fact, she has merrily diverted him from his scientific gambling to more individual pleasures. Through Phillips's love of money, sensuosity (a potential threat to Christian maidens), and experimentalizing, Frankau establishes his degeneration.

Furthermore, Frankau asserts that Phillips's Jewishness emerges in his anxiety over money. He willingly supports two households, "but he was always and above all things a Jew, and he could not see the balance at his banker's running low without anxiety" (104). When Phillips speculates rashly on the Stock Exchange and financially ruins himself, he worries about losing his mistress, but his major anxiety is financial ruin: "His money troubles—so strong were his race instincts—pressed upon him the hardest" (229). Frankau consistently links Phillips's Jewishness to his desire for money and to his character in general, as when she comments, "But for his race training and instincts, all would have been good [in the man]" (109).

Phillips's corruption is not yet complete. Frankau examines each step he takes along the path he follows. Once he learns of his financial ruin, Phillips's pride keeps him from requesting money to keep his mistress from his wife. Knowing he is the beneficiary of his wife's will, Phillips kills her, and Frankau casually dismisses the irony of his killing his wife rather than asking for her cash. Ultimately, he loses his mistress as well as his practice and becomes first a pariah of the Jewish community, "his Jewish patients . . .

deserted him" (335), and then a Jew-hater. Phillips "watched them [former friends] pass him one by one, and found comfort in noting the ugliness of their walk, the brilliancy of their cherished Sabbath clothes, and smug satisfaction which glistened greasily on their coarse features and loose lips" (336). As he watches he grows bitter and resentful: "It wounded him doubly, that they could wound him, these people who were so immeasurably inferior to him, and whom he could even despise" (336). Phillips recognizes himself "as the outcast Jew. The Jew who—though a larger world may honour him, and his name be much in the mouths of men—is yet cast out from the hearts of his people" (336—37).

Unable to accept this treatment, Phillips allows his resentment to grow,

and Benjamin Phillips . . . from the outcast Jew, became in time the Jew-hater. Apart from them, he began to see their faults more clearly; their virtues, the clannishness, hospitality, generosity, of which he had used to boast, when no longer practiced towards himself, were obliterated by their bigotry, their narrowness, their greed. (337)

Phillips's hate apparently—for at this juncture the narrator disclaims close knowledge—becomes disinterest. Ten years later,

his Judaism has fallen from him like a discarded garment; he is scarcely known as an Israelite; he scarcely acknowledges the title. What he suffered, or whether he suffered in that separation, he confided to no one. . . . He dwells in honour among his contemporaries, an outcast from his people, outwardly happy. (339—40)

The character of Dr. Phillips illustrates at length Frankau's attitude toward the Jew whose God is gain and, therefore, whose character is thoroughly undermined by what money can buy. Because Phillips is morally bankrupt, when he openly sheds his religion, his medical purpose is "to unsex women and maim men; to be a living testimony of manual dexterity and moral recklessness" (341). Like other nominal Jews portrayed by Anglo-Jewish novelists, Phillips is cast morally adrift.

Perhaps Phillips's idol is Mammon because he came from a poor family, although Frankau does not present his background. She does suggest that the other, now prosperous, Jews in the novel came from poor homes. They share Phillips's worship of Mammon, but they do not gamble on the Stock Exchange. Equally important, through them Frankau illustrates various levels of the Jewish social scale. These levels, she indicates, are determined by their social ambition, which in turn is based on whether or not they accept Christians. They live in neighborhoods comprised only of Jews:

In a sort of jealous exclusiveness these Jews lived by and among themselves. They fancied they did so from choice. It was not so: it was a remnant of the times when the yellow cap and curiously-shaped gaberdine marked them out as lepers in the crowd. The garb had been discarded, but the shrinking feeling of generations was still lingering. There is a certain pride in these people; they are at once the creatures and the outcasts of civilisation. (60)

They live in ghettolike neighborhoods, yet these Jews do not freely associate with each other. Instead, they divide themselves into castes. The leaders of one caste, the more socially ambitious and accultured Jews, lionize Christians.

Frankau concentrates on the women of this caste, among whom Mrs. Detmar is the leader because her wealth exceeds that of the others. Mrs. Detmar

saw herself as the centre about which all things ought to revolve. If people persisted in forsaking this orbit of revolution, she bore them little malice; but she considered them eccentric, not to say mad. As a girl, she had desired to make a wealthy marriage, and had succeeded. As a woman, she desired to have a circle sufficiently large to enable her to play cards at a different house every night of the week; to be richer than anyone she played with, and in a position to give better suppers. She had succeeded in all these, and, in a good-natured way, wished to help others on to similar fortunes. (58–59)

Befitting their social status in their group, the Detmars accept a Christian woman as if "they had known her from childhood" (68).

Other members of the group, the Jeddingtons, are perhaps more socially ambitious than the Detmars. They exemplify the upwardly mobile Jew who is clannish but also socially bigoted. Mr. Jeddington,

whose original name had been Moses, had made his enormous fortune by selling ready-made and second-hand clothing to the Colonies. Now they were socially ambitious: they belonged to that class of Jews who see in every Christian a probable "swell," in every Jew a direct descendant of an old clothes-man or a hawker. (9)

Because the Jeddingtons disdain Jews for their humble origins, they have no objection to their daughter's mingling with Christians. The result is that the Jeddington's daughter comes to believe that Christians "have much better style than our people" (10). Another member of this group, Mrs. Collings, is less upwardly mobile, as typified by her clannishness. Mrs. Collings

felt it would be abjuring the creed of her life to allow a heretic to enter into intimacy. Public opinion, expedience, and a certain sheep-like habit of following, had led her to admit a few Christian men to her dances. . . . But when it came to women, she felt it her bounden duty to protest. She actually believed all women, except those of her own race, to be unchaste. (61)

In their headlong rush to the social heights, these Jews are neither constrained nor motivated by religion but by being better than everyone else.

That these women's values are false, Frankau illustrates in two ways. First the Christian woman they "adopt" reveals her true feelings about her supposedly dear friends:

"Jews, Jews!" she almost hissed this out. "The scum of civilization, I know you now! Money-dogs! pedlars, sharps. You—your company has degraded me, me, me!! Do you hear? Jews!" Nothing can express the scorn with which she uttered the word "Jews." (204)

The direct vituperation with which she faces them in a moment of revelatory anger indicates the naiveté and foolishness with which the Jewish women have acted in esteeming her before they knew her.

Second, Frankau shows her disapproval of their values by belittling these women. They are physically ugly, mentally empty, and they spend their time frivolously—playing cards. (These women appear to be in the tradition of the upper middle-class card-playing females in Jane Austen's novels.) Their affinity for playing cards outweighs social distinctions among them; on this trivial expenditure of time the narrator concentrates. These "heavy, coarse-featured, narrow-minded Jewesses" (168) vacation together and "are very gregarious. They separate at luncheon, certainly; and many of them take that meal with their children; but after luncheon they meet again in parties of threes and fours in each other's houses and play cards" (144). Frankau belittles these women for wasting their lives, and she suggests they are materialistic robots, as when she summarizes their mode of existence:

all the burning questions of the hour are to them a dead letter; art, literature and politics exist not for them. They have but one aim, the acquisition of wealth. Playing cards at each other's houses is their sole experience of the charms of social intercourse; their interests are bounded by their homes and those of their neighbouring brethren. (168)

Frankau's community of Jews, united by their interests in making money and in card-playing, differs little from Levy's. Levy's community also aims to accumulate wealth but her women spend their time gossiping rather than playing cards. Both novelists follow their major characters to show what befalls Jews whose sole interest continues to be financial gain, and both utilize a surrounding community to elaborate on their theme. Frankau spends more time in *Dr. Phillips* on her community, repeatedly showing exactly how accultured middle-class Jewish women waste their lives, but *Reuben Sachs* and *Dr. Phillips* are similar in their illustrations of human dissipation.

The Anglo-Jewish novelists' portrayal of Jews who yield to the pressures of assimilation cannot escape comparison with negative Victorian portraits of Jews. Levy, Frankau, and their English contemporaries concentrate on the Jewish quest for money as much as on that for social status. Anglo-Jewish novelists add more of the flavoring of Judaism through descriptions of festivals and rituals, and they are specifically scornful of women who waste their time. They also depict Jewish men in a denigrating manner. Whether these men rise from street hawking or inherit their fortunes, whether their charity is notable or their shrewdness notorious, whether they emerge as family men or possess no respect for women, whether they hypocritically retain their Orthodoxy or their ascendance on the social scale encourages a proportionate decline in religious observance, Anglo-Jews who acculture or assimilate are generally shown to possess an affinity for amassing money which unites them in a vulgar brotherhood of wealth. Harris presents the pressures to assimilate and intermarry without criticism. Levy and Frankau criticize and lamentably remain on the level of their more virulent English counterparts by extending their criticism of their poor examples to stand for all Jews.

Levy and Frankau's treatment of Jews indicates some of the

problems inherent in defining how to be a good Jew at the end of the nineteenth century as well as the novelists' increasing discontent with a particular section of the Anglo-Jewish community. Their criticism of Jews manifests itself differently from their criticism or acknowledgement of Christian anti-Semitism. Levy and Frankau link particular negative qualities belonging to individual characters to *all* Jews. They do not generalize in this way about Christians. The distinction in treatment does not mean that these Anglo-Jewish novelists fear to offend Christian readers, rather that they concern themselves more with fellow Jews and that their scorn for the materialistic Jew spills over and sullies all Jews. (Levy and Frankau's scorn of fellow Jews foreshadows the quality of Jewish self-hatred which informs a portion of twentieth-century Jewish literature in which the accultured Jew is alienated from Judaism and Jewish society and may even identify with the oppressor.) Moreover, despite some overt hostility in their fiction to their own community, these novelists appear to be staunch Jews who want to correct what they perceive as errors.

Novels written during the last third of the century show Anglo-Jews beginning to recognize the world beyond Judaism, generally for the wrong reasons: to satisfy one's ambitions, as most of the characters discussed in this chapter do, or to try and live honorably among Christians as Farjeon's Aaron Cohen (*Aaron the Jew*, 1894) does. Late Victorian Anglo-Jews step out of their "tribal duckpond" (*Reuben Sachs*, 37), however, to face some Christian and Jewish hostility; they attempt to move beyond the fact of anti-Semitism and to define for themselves what being Jewish means and how to be Jewish in a Christian society.

CHAPTER 6

The Challenge from Within: Immigration

FOR many nineteenth-century immigrant Jews, the transition
from a restricted ghetto life to that in a liberal country was sharp
and sometimes difficult. Until the last two decades of Victoria's
reign, Anglo-Jews integrated immigrants into various Anglo-Jewish
communities and thus helped their coreligionists make the change—
an easy task when only two to four hundred immigrants a year were
arriving in England. Most of the immigrants gladly acknowledged
their Judaism. Those that did not were still marked because of their
religion. The Christian society could and sometimes did make Jews
uncomfortably aware they were Jews and immigrants. Likewise, the
immigrants made some Anglo-Jews uncomfortable. For at least one
early Anglo-Jewish novelist, Samuel Phillips, integration of the
immigrant was not effected quickly enough. He depicts the immigrant Jewish moneylender in a tone which reflects his annoyance
that some Jews were not learning to behave in the proper English
manner.

Because of the numbers, later immigrants were less easily accom-
modated in the existing Anglo-Jewish communities. The 100,000
new arrivals between 1881 and 1905 created a major problem, one
which threatened to split the Anglo-Jewish community (Lipman,
Social History, 90). By 1900 approximately 150,000 Jews lived in
London alone, almost two-thirds were émigrés clustered in the East
End. Of the approximately 60,000 Jews in England in the 1880s,
more than one half were born in England (Lipman, *Three Centuries*,
107). The more acculturated of this group were repelled by the lower-
class immigrants. These immigrants threatened to outnumber earlier arrivals. In contrast to other Anglo-Jews, the Anglo-Jewish
novelists who wrote scornfully about the immigrants made little
distinction between East European Jews and German Jews, who

were accepted more readily than their Slavic brethren. While Israel Zangwill sympathetically examines Jews living in the East End, Julia Frankau, who also wrote about Jewish immigrants, makes clear her displeasure with immigrant Jews who tried to push themselves into English society before they learned proper English manners. Hers is not a very different view from that of Samuel Phillips, who had expressed his revulsion at the dirty dishonest immigrant as early as 1842. Neither Frankau nor Phillips indicates the countries from which their characters emigrate.

I *Samuel Phillips*

Samuel Phillips (1815—1854) is the only novelist of those under discussion here whose Judaism cannot be finally established. Calisch lists Phillips as a Jew in his bibliography. An English bookseller, Harold Mortlake, believes Phillips may have converted to Christianity.[1] In the absence of a final source to confirm either position or add any other information and in consideration of Calisch's published, positive assertion as well as his closer chronological proximity, Phillips is included as an Anglo-Jewish novelist. An essayist and editor of the *Literary Gazette*, Phillips wrote one novel, a volume of short stories, and three other stories published in *Blackwood's* between 1846 and 1853.[2] Phillips denigrates Jews in one short story, "Moses and Son" (*Blackwood's*, 1846), and at length in his novel, *Caleb Stukely*.

Caleb Stukely began appearing in *Blackwood's* in 1842. In book form *Caleb Stukely* appeared in three English editions, in 1844, 1854, and 1862, and in an American edition in 1843. This novel added to the literature a portrayal of Jews in no way different from anti-Semitic English portrayals. A first-person narrative, *Caleb Stukely* describes an innocent and gullible young man's initiation into a world of felons, including a Jewish moneylender and his son. These depictions are included in an offhand manner, as if the only moneylenders near Trinity College from 1795 to 1797 were dirty, crafty, and Jewish. Solomon Levy and his associates have no relation to the community other than lending money, and they apparently do business only to take advantage of others. Because Levy and his men, unlike other characters in the novel, appear exclusively as parasites, they are the most negative depictions.

Like many of the negative English portraits of Jews, Solomon Levy has "glossy and black curly hair. . . . [and] vivacity and fire [in his] eye which moved with the quickness and sharpness of youth."[3] Innocent as Caleb supposedly is, he knows enough to link Levy's physical dirtiness with his religion:

His whole person was characterized by dirtiness. His face, hands, (he wore no gloves,) clothes, and boots, all were dirty. . . . The complexion of this curious person was a dark brown, and looked the browner by reason of his universal fault. . . . and all his features were strongly stamped with that peculiar expression which is recognized all over the world under the name of—Jewish. (51, 232)

Levy's family is equally dirty and so is his home: "Like the great proprietor, [his house] boasted of its dirt. Mud, dirt, and filth were heaped upon it" (51, 591).

The portrait of Levy resembles other negative depictions in its characterization of the moneylender as a hypocrite, replete with stage accent. Levy presents himself to Caleb as a friend: " 'Vy do I live, Mr. Stukely, in this vorld of trouble?—only to oblige my friends' " (51, 590). Less than an acquaintance, the obsequious Levy deliberately dupes Caleb with protestations of friendship. When the deluded Caleb applies for a loan, Levy first pretends he has no money, savors Caleb's distress, and then mysteriously raises seventy pounds in gold and thirty pounds in port, a commodity Levy sells. For this he exacts as security Caleb's mother's gold watch and all his "goods and chattel" (51, 596). When Levy later tries to collect on that loan, he reveals his thorough duplicity. Levy asks a friend to perjure himself in court. When that friend is found out and arrested, Levy disappears.

Unlike most negative depictions of Jews, the cunning Levy shuns outward displays of wealth and cares little for social advancement. His interests lie in cozening loan applicants and in training his eldest son, Ikey, who is already adept at hustling such gullibles as Caleb. Caleb describes Ikey as

the father's pride, Levy's son and heir, his better self—his youthful Prince of Wales—on whom the parent's mantle must descend—in whom the father's brightest hopes are fixed. His body is twelve years old, his head a hundred. There is more knowledge of the human creature—of the impure gross part, that lies hidden in the soul's corrupted sink—written and engraved in that precocious cunning cheek, than twenty ordinary men can boast. (51, 592)

When Caleb applies for a loan, Ikey melodramatically offsets his father's pretended willingness to lend money: " 'What's the use of your asking [how much Caleb needs?]' shrieked the young monster. 'You know you haven't a shilling in the house' " (51, 593). Ikey's words produce in Caleb "awful abdominal pains" (51, 593), and then the father and son begin earnestly to prolong Caleb's distress until he accepts the loan on the elder Levy's terms.

Ikey Levy fulfills his father's pride in him. He wittily upsets the lawyer defending Caleb, and at the story's end he lives in a "stylish house" with a barouche at the door and the gaudiest appointments inside. Moreover,

he seems dressed in livery himself. . . . Gold chains across his breast . . . and on every finger sparkles a precious jewel. Thick mustaches and a thicker beard adorn the foreign face; but a certain air which it assumes, convinces you without delay that it is the property of an unmitigated blackguard . . . [who] has made good the promises of his childhood and his youth. He rolls in riches, and is—a fashionable money-lender. (53, 672)

Other blackguards appear in the novel; they relate to Caleb in more ways than have the Levys, however. Solomon Levy pushes himself forward as a friend but acts only as a crafty usurer, training his son to be the same. Because they alone are viewed only in one role, it appears that the narrator uses them to comment negatively on Jewish moneylenders. At the very least the elder Levy bears a strong resemblance to Dickens's Fagin, who also presents himself as a friend for his own avaricious purposes.

Whereas most negative depictions of Jews do not include detailed accounts of the practice of Judaism (to show a man praying might be to humanize him), Phillips's account of Levy at his prayers, placed in the Christian Caleb's mouth, is accurate and detailed:

Before him was a Hebrew book; upon his forehead, exactly between his eyes, a small square piece of leather-covered wood, (so it appeared to me,) kept in its position by a leathern thong, which running through a loop was carried round the head and tied behind. His left arm was exposed. Around it some dozen times was strapped another thong, similar to that about his head. His coat was off; his vest unbuttoned; over the once white shirt he wore a curious coloured garment, formed of two square pieces of blue cloth, one hanging down before his breast, the other to his back, and both attached by means of two long slips of tape connecting them. At the extremity of the four corners were long fringes of white worsted, fastened in small knots. The fringes in the front were in Mr. Levy's grasp when I walked in, and started with amazement at the novel spectacle. (51, 591)

Levy interrupts his prayers to greet Caleb, saying, " 'You don't disturb me in the least. I know it all by heart. I'm only saying my prayers' " (51, 591). He subsequently interrupts these prayers repeatedly to question Caleb, to discipline his children and wife, to address Caleb again, and finally, "once more in ecstasy he wiped his visage with the fringes, and kissed them passionately; and last of all, he turned his face towards the wall, bowed to it with reverence repeatedly, and beat his breast with force and sound that would have pleased a stethoscopist's ear" (51, 592−93). Caleb's earlier amazement is replaced by curiosity and the comment, after a few of Levy's interruptions, that "his compliance with the [Jewish] law was evidently irksome" (51, 592).

The external description of Judaism, if not the negative tone, is appropriate here because a non-Jewish narrator describes Levy at prayer. Levy prays in the Orthodox fashion and wears ritual aids to prayer—phylacteries and *tzitzis*—but his ultimate connection with Judaism remains unclear. Caleb Stukely describes Levy throughout, and no statement of Levy's counteracts Caleb's about the moneylender's religious laxity. The author himself gives scant attention to Jewish rituals and thereby reinforces Caleb's negative comment about Jewish moneylenders. Through this technique Phillips advances his disparaging portrayal. If Levy's prayers are superficial, the conclusion must be that he uses Judaism as a guise of piety. If he genuinely prays, he practices in his work a philosophy opposite to his religion or at best distinctly separates the two areas of his life and, therefore, is not a devout Jew. In either case the characterization of Levy, the cunning moneylender, is a portrait of the hypocrite, gleefully tricking others, training his son to do the same, and, unlike Farjeon's Solomon Isaacs, finding unlimited success. It appears that Phillips permits Solomon Levy to get away with his scurrilous dealings because, at the very least, the novelist disdained immigrant Jewish moneylenders who were also blackguards.

In addition, Caleb's description of Levy at prayer differs in no large manner from Aguilar's externalized descriptions of rituals. Aguilar's Jewish narrator calls the rituals "peculiar" or "mysterious" and fails to explain them; this non-Jewish narrator grasps only the surface impression of a Jew praying. Caleb's impression of Levy at his prayers underlines Aguilar's externalized view of Judaism. The difference between the two novelists' technique lies in their purposes. Aguilar's narrator pleads for refined English feelings about Jews; Phillips's Caleb reinforces negative Victorian notions about dishonest immigrant Jewish moneylenders.

Like Phillips, Julia Frankau expressed her revulsion at the
immigrants. Three of her four novels with Jewish characters dispar-
age them. In her second novel, *A Babe in Bohemia* (1889), which saw
three English editions but was not published in this country, there is
only one, very minor Jewish character. An immigrant singer from
Italy, now living in Whitechapel, Signor Antonelli makes a brief
appearance in this novel, which relates an innocent girl's introduction to bohemian life in London. Frankau appraises Antonelli
mockingly not only because his performance is histrionic but also
because he lisps and has an inferior voice: "The bearded, rolling-
eyed young Jew gave out the familiar words with a thrilling
unctuousness of love. . . . But, alas, as the softened r's rolled out of his
thick-lipped mouth, he called it 'bweast,' and above the delicious
pathos rang the yet more melancholy circumstance of a defective
upper register."[4] As she does in *Dr. Phillips*, Frankau links the Jew's
defects to his Judaism, here using that technique to denigrate the
immigrant.

In her third novel with Jewish characters, *Pigs in Clover* (1903),
Frankau examines first generation Anglo-Jews who try to assimilate.
Set in 1895, this novel was published once in England and four times
in America. The problem of *Pigs in Clover* is that two Jewish brothers
want to be accepted into the nonreceptive English aristocratic
society. Wealthy Victorians in this novel govern themselves by an
all-encompassing code of exclusiveness, prohibiting the " 'pigs in
clover' element [from] intrud[ing] into the circle, where . . . blood
should have been the only credential."[5] It matters not "whether they
professed the religion of the country they inhabited, or whether they
acknowledged, if they did not conform to, the restrictions of a more
ancient faith" (60−61). To exclude the "*nouveaux riches*" is their
obsession and social crusade (62). Although these aristocrats dislike
all upstarts, the ones to receive their opprobrium are Jews. When
an Englishman believes Jews misused him, it is their faith he curses
along with them: "He had cursed the Althauses, root and branch,
their race, and everybody connected with them" (296). Frankau
glosses this Englishman's reaction: "It is the misfortune of the Jews
that one of their community cannot misbehave without earning
opprobrium for their whole body. The prejudice is still very vivid
and real, however it may be glozed over by civilized thought and
cultivated reason" (296).

In spite of her apparent sympathy, Frankau portrays the brothers,
Karl and Louis Althaus, severely and disapprovingly. Karl Althaus,
a self-made millionaire and an avowedly dishonest businessman,

was raised as a Jew, but he renounces his religion. He admits, " 'I am a Jew by birth, by instinct, by sympathy. Judaism is . . . part of myself, the best part' " (105). Despite this knowledge, Karl exiles himself from his religion when his paralyzed mother, whom he has lovingly tended, dies and his callous neighbors console him with words about his new freedom:

> The Jewish women who came from the synagogue muttered their prayers in Hebrew, but showed the poor body no respect when they took it from the bed. They made an alien of him. . . . The neighbors who in all kindliness said to him: "It's a good thing she's gone; now you'll be free," made an exile of him from the quarter. He had loved his burden, hugged it to him, never forgot how she had worked for him. (116)

Alienated for years, Karl now believes Judaism to be a "thing of forms and food, a race habit. There's no religion in it" (106); but neither can he accept Christ, although he would like to. Unable to convert, Karl wants to expose the Jew to Christ: "I'd like to keep every custom and habit and ceremony he's got, but I'd like him to know about Christ" (108). "Ineradicably a Jew and an unbeliever" (362), Karl fruitlessly schemes to impart knowledge of Christ to Jews primarily by building a theater which would first court Jews with performances of Bible stories and then proselytize by presenting the story of Christ. For Harris's once Orthodox Benedictus and for the assimilated Karl the result is identical: in reaction to their coreligionists' unresponsiveness and insensitivity, both alienate themselves from and are lost to Judaism.

Like Gordon and Farjeon, Frankau shows that a Jew cannot fully escape his religious origins. Karl cannot renounce his generosity to others and his family loyalty, both of which appear in this novel as the flowering of his Jewish heritage. He gives money freely to those in need. He takes care of his wily, shallow half-brother, Louis, a venal man whose greed has left him bereft of human companionship. But Karl cannot straighten out his own personal life, and Frankau establishes the cause to be his lack of an ethical underpinning.

Frankau's characterization of the brothers indicates little sympathy for assimilated Jews. Her portrait of the repulsive Louis is close to the negative English stereotype, that of Karl similar. She shows Karl using dishonest business methods he learned in Whitechapel and has him admit that he does "not know the meaning of honesty" (117). Karl's redeeming qualities, no doubt, are those which make him yearn for Christianity, like the Jews in conversionist novels.

This depiction of the "good-bad" Jew is, in effect, even more negative than the stereotype. Moreover, although Frankau demonstrates that a Jew cannot escape his Jewishness, for her that is not a positive trait. Like Levy, Frankau links her Jews to all with derogatory comments, as when she calls Louis, "the descendant of that wheedling, ringleted son of a race that is no longer a nation" (142), and says of the inscription on Karl's mother's tombstone, it was "in some strange lettering that [Jews] could not read" (324). As in *Dr. Phillips*, Frankau's target is the Jew who aims to amass money and break into society by leaving Judaism behind. That her criticism does not stop at individual Jews vitiates the protest she makes in the preface to the second edition of *Dr. Phillips*. Not simply a portion of the community but all Jews receive Frankau's hostility.

Perhaps all Jews receive Frankau's opprobrium because she, like Levy, sees Orthodox Jews as insensitive. Frankau also views nominal Jews as deliberately materialistic, dishonest, and vulgar. Assuredly, that is so in her last novel about Jews, *The Sphinx's Lawyer* (1906), which was simultaneously published in England and America. In this novel Frankau spotlights Jews who have yielded fully to the pressures of English society, who have assimilated without formally converting but who are lost to the Jewish community nonetheless. Unlike the English community in *Pigs in Clover*, the English community in *The Sphinx's Lawyer*, except for one man married to a Jew, accepts Jews on their merits as people. Frankau's negative opinion of assimilated Jews appears in her characterization of her Jewish community. It consists of two self-made businessmen, Sam Beethoven and Manny Henry, who anglicize their names and believe they can buy anything they want; Sam's wife, Elsa, an adulterous opportunist; and Manny's daughter, Lily, who marries an English anti-Semite her father "bought" her.

Frankau depicts the men as Trollope had over thirty years before. Beethoven and Henry are dirty, they have heavy accents, and they are vulgar. Henry is unwilling to take no for an answer, as when he forces his way past a clerk into a lawyer's office, yelling, "I didn't get there [to wealth] by waiting on clerks."[6] About the women Frankau is scarcely more complementary. Elsa Beethoven wants to run away from her husband and marry her English lover. Prevented by his sister, for a long while Elsa plans revenge, but she finally returns to the weak, forgiving Sam. Lily du Gore, née Henry, is "intelligent, companionable, eager and quick to learn" (245), but she is also weak. Frankau concentrates on Lily's marriage to Kenny du Gore, a poor lying English aristocrat who calls Lily a "prig in petticoats" (194–95) because she disapproves of his imitations of her father. Their marriage endures three separations, the last when Kenny accuses Lily of dressing their son "up like a damn little Jew Boy" and of teaching him "he ought to be quite as proud he'd got Jew ancestors, as of the du Gores" (199). Through these separations Lily is torn between her love for Kenny and her dislike of his malicious jeering. Their marriage seems irreparably ruptured when Kenny accidently kills their son, but with the aid of non-Jewish friends, Kenny and Lily get the opportunity at the end of the novel to "begin again" (374). That the du Gores receive aid from Christians rather than Jews suggests Frankau's belief—indicated in all four of her novels under discussion here—that Jews can give primarily monetary assistance. When money cannot be useful, they do not know what to do. Money is what Manny Henry uses. He tries to buy Lily's way out of the marriage; when that fails and his grandson dies, Henry keeps Kenny from Lily with lies instead of listening to her pleas for her husband. Frankau characterizes Jews negatively in this novel by depicting them as vulgar upstarts who believe money to be the only important thing in life and also by showing their helplessness in relation to Christian Englishmen. While Phillips disguises his scorn of the immigrant Jew by placing it in the Christian Caleb's mouth, Frankau speaks directly. No less than Phillips's Solomon Levy are her immigrants to be scorned— Antonelli for his lisp and inferior voice, Louis Althaus for his venal grasping, Karl for his inability to be honest and of one religion, and the Jews in *The Sphinx's Lawyer* because they are assimilated vulgarians.

II *Israel Zangwill*

Short-story writer, playwright, essayist, novelist, lecturer, and polemicist, Israel Zangwill (1864–1926) was also a political figure. Born in Whitechapel, the son of a peddler, Zangwill received his education at the Jews' Free School. He became, along with Theodore Herzl, the champion of a homeland for Jews, although unlike Herzl, Zangwill did not believe Palestine was necessarily the place. Zangwill's brother Louis (1869–1938) wrote novels, none of which deals with Jews, about English life and culture under the pseudonym ZZ; his son Oliver (1913–) has written scientific books and has also been a professor of experimental psychology at Cambridge. Until

1907, when he devoted himself to politics, Zangwill wrote twelve novels including mysteries, three plays, two volumes of essays about Judaism, two volumes of poetry, and four volumes of short stories as well as innumerable pamphlets about Judaism. Of his fiction, three volumes of short stories and two novels deal with Jews.[7] Throughout these works runs the dilemma of Jews outside of the ghetto and without a homeland: how much Judaism should one retain. Those who discarded their religion Zangwill sketches in *Dreamers of the Ghetto* (1898), showing how historical figures like the poet Heine, the philosopher Spinoza, and the prime minister Disraeli, assimilated to Christian society but retained Jewish qualities, as when Disraeli in "The Primrose Sphinx" is seen to have the self-mastery of the ghetto Jew, whose heart is with his people and who is linked by way of Judaism to all people, but who keeps his secret. A popular book, *Dreamers of the Ghetto* was published twice in America, once in England, and was translated into German and into three different French editions.

In his short stories Zangwill contrasts the tragic and comic aspects of ghetto life. In *Ghetto Tragedies* (1893), which went through three English and two American editions and which was subsequently republished three times in America as *They That Walk in Darkness* (1899), he examines the difficulties inherent in remaining true or in being false to Judaism. In "Transitional," Florence, the youngest of seven daughters, determines to marry a Christian but only after her Orthodox father dies. In order not to hinder her happiness, her father decides to accept the marriage in order to see his daughter happy while he lives. Florence discovers her father's real feeling—he cannot go along with her plans—and renounces her intended, writing, "Perhaps the prosaic epoch of Judaism . . . is only transitional . . . perhaps the future will redevelop . . . [Judaism's] diviner sides."[8] Florence's self-abnegation, modeled on her father's, prevents her earthly happiness. Ironically, her living out this abnegation shows her being true to a Christian principle.

In a different way, being false to Judaism brings its own ironies. Talented Isaac Levinsky, in "To Die in Jerusalem," runs away from home, anglicizes his name, and becomes a renowned playwright, cutting himself from the "swaddling coils" (171) of Judaism. His mother dies without a last glimpse of her son. His father, once an eloquent preacher, sees his life in ruins and decides to attain an Orthodox Jewish wish—to die in Jerusalem. Learning that Isaac is dying, from Jerusalem the old man writes to pardon his son for leaving Judaism but instead returns to England to bless Isaac. In vain has the preacher undertaken the journey. In hopes of receiving his father's blessing, Isaac the assimilated Jew, travels to Jerusalem and dies, while the old Orthodox Jew, spent and ill, dies in London.

Subjects only somewhat lighter than death form the substance of *Ghetto Comedies* (1907), published once in England, twice in America, and translated into German. In this volume Zangwill focuses mainly on the anguish of immigrant Jews as some transgress Jewish law in their haste to become more English. "The Sabbath Question in Sudminster," for example, relates the story of the pious Sudminster congregation. Members of the congregation are enraged that the new member, Simeon Samuels the marine dealer, religiously attends both Friday evening and Saturday morning services but also keeps his shop open on the Sabbath in defiance of Jewish law. The preacher suggests from the pulpit that Samuels close his shop on the Sabbath. Samuels ignores him. Various prominent Jews of the synagogue try to reason with Samuels, but they wind up either buying an item they cannot use or being outreasoned. Realizing that Samuels is making more money by keeping longer hours than the other Jewish merchants in the community and so underselling them, these merchants buy out Samuels on the condition that he leave town. Samuels leaves for London but only to restock his store. Aghast and threatened with a split in the synagogue, the merchants try a homeopathic cure—they keep their shops open on the Sabbath. Their success is twofold: it drives Samuels "in search of a more pious seaport," where he can again undersell his Jewish competitors, and it keeps Sudminster Jews in synagogue on the Sabbath "listening reverentially . . . while its shops are engaged in supplying the wants of Christendom."[9] Zangwill shows that the legal and emotional complexities of Judaism force many Jews to live and die in ways other than they would choose.

While the short stories poignantly reveal the difficult decisions immigrant Jews must make, it is Zangwill's earliest and longest work of fiction on Judaism, *Children of the Ghetto: A Study of a Peculiar People* (1892) that concentrates on Judaism and the problem of "dwindling Orthodoxy" in England. Zangwill here portrays Judaism without the ghetto walls but within the light of contemporary skepticism. This was Zangwill's most popular work of fiction. It saw five English editions, four American editions (the last in 1938), and was translated into German. Zangwill contrasts older Jews' devotion to their religious past, in the way they live and pray in the English "ghetto"—a devotion he sees without a future—with younger Jews' efforts to remove themselves from this "ghetto" as well as, in many cases, Judaism because of its restrictiveness. Zangwill examines the problem not by disdaining either group but by sympathetically portraying the gap between older and younger Jews as one which arises within families. He sees the separation between parent and child in England as brought about by the possibility of change in religious adherence, as he explains, the new generation was quietly but steadily drifting away "from the old landmarks. The synagogue did not attract; it spoke Hebrew to those whose mother-tongue was English . . . it was out of touch with their real lives; its liturgy prayed for the restoration of sacrifices which they did not want. . . . Practically, [Jews were] without religion" (439).

Essentially a series of vignettes examining the types of Jews living in the East End, *Children of the Ghetto* follows the growth of children who rebel against their parents' Orthodoxy and scrutinizes the forces behind the rebellions. In one instance the parents rebel against their children. Daniel and Hannah Hyams grow up in England and are secretly ashamed of their Orthodox, foreign parents who divine the truth. The elder Hyams concludes he must leave his children and go to America, reasoning "if it stands written that I must break with my children, let the gap be too wide for repining" (214). He and his wife leave and free their son to marry the girl he loves.

Six other examples in the novel portray the degrees to which Orthodox children shake off their Judaism. Esther Ansell, the daughter of pious but penniless Moses Ansell, grows up in a poor Orthodox household and as a child is "pious to the point of fanaticism" (102). As she learns English history, she grows prouder of her English heritage than of her Jewish descent. Adopted by a wealthy middle-class family when her own leaves for America, Esther writes a scathing novel about English Jews and remains firm in her belief that Jews "have no ideals now" (340) and that Judaism is intellectually dead. (While Zangwill asserted that the portrait of Esther was himself, his depiction may also be based on the career of Amy Levy.) Not until she is persuaded to write for an Orthodox newspaper and is ripened by her knowledge of her religion, does Esther drop her skepticism and come to believe in Judaism again.

Hannah Jacobs, daughter of a rabbi, drops her already weak adherence to Judaism when an ironic joke marries her to a man she does not love and an obscure Jewish law forbids her marriage to

David Brandon, the man she does love. Knowing that her father will consider her dead if she marries Brandon, Hannah ultimately refuses the young man. Reverend Joseph Strelitski, persecuted as a child in Russia, is an ardent Zionist as a young man. He assumes the pulpit of a wealthy Orthodox congregation only to become disenchanted with Orthodoxy, which he discovers "is inextricably entangled with ritual observance; and ceremonial religion is of the ancient world, not the modern" (510). Strelitski resigns to go to America, idealistically believing Jews can do more for the world without a mother country but with a mother tongue, as Zangwill himself asserted.

Esther, Hannah, and Strelitski exemplify Jews who rebel against their parents and are caught up in the late nineteenth-century argument about modification of Jewish rituals, ideals, and aims. Other characters examplify the Jew who loses his heart to the wider world and severs himself from his brethren. Sidney Graham and Percy Saville anglicize their names. Graham changes into an "avowed infidel in a world where avowal is the unpardonable sin. He did not even pretend to fast on the Day of Atonement" (325). Instead, he asks, " 'Why should I subject myself to petty martyrdom for the sake of an outworn creed and a decaying sect?' " (407). Levi Jacobs, Hannah's brother, changes his name to Leonard James, explaining, " 'I'm not fitted for the narrow life that suits my father and mother and my sister. They've got no ideas beyond the house, and religion, and all that sort of thing. What do you think my father wanted me to be? A minister! Think of it! Ha! ha! ha! Me a minister!' " (413). Now James eats pork, attends law school, and intends to become an actor. His father, a rabbi, sees his son violate the Passover by "coming out of an unclean place . . . with the 'strange woman' of the *Proverbs*, for whom the faithful Jew has a hereditary hatred" (434); and he considers his son to be dead before James shakes his father off as " 'only an old Jew who supplies me with cash' " (435).

These six young adults who range in belief from Orthodoxy to no formal religion illustrate simultaneously the generation gap between parent and child and the movement away from Orthodox adherence. Although a few, like Esther and Strelitski, make some kind of peace with their parents and their religion, the majority do not. These characters, questing even in their rebellion, are very different from Marie Morales (*The Vale of Cedars*), whose father's word is law and whose religion in every detail is sacred. These later characters reflect Jewish acculturation or assimilation to English society, present even among the more Orthodox Jews at the end of the Victorian era. With waning Orthodoxy there is proportionally waning support for family life and more inclination to strike out on one's own.

Zangwill knew the power of Judaism as a revealed religion, but he also perceived it as intellectually dead and believed that Judaism would eventually blend with Christianity for its betterment (Fisch, 930). Perhaps that is the reason Zangwill set *The King of Schnorrers* (1894) at the end of the eighteenth century when, he apparently trusted, most Jews practiced their religion and few, even in England, chafed under religious restrictions. His wittiest work, *The King of Schnorrers*, was not only adapted for the stage but was published four times in England, three times in America, once in Canada, and was translated into French and Italian. This work also gave the title to a volume of short stories (1894), which does not present only Jewish characters.

Like the short stories and *Children of the Ghetto*, this novel has an intellectual foundation. Jewish tradition and teaching prize education and charity. Even a society divided into the very rich, which could afford the two, and the very poor, which generally could not, esteemed both highly. In *The King of Schnorrers* Zangwill shows how one of the very poor and therefore supposedly ignorant, a Sephardic beggar by the name of Manasseh Bueno Barzillai Azevedo da Costa, capably outwits an Ashkenazic millionaire, Joseph Grobstock, in addition to various other townspeople and the pompous officers of his own Sephardic synagogue—all by employing his vast knowledge of Judaism and Jewish teachings. Da Costa is not an ordinary beggar but a *schnorrer*. The Yiddish word suggests audacity and guile without falsehood; at the same time it signifies style. Indeed, in his assisting wealthy Jews to discharge their religious obligations to charity—from money to clothes to an evening at the theater or a dinner—da Costa is unsurpassed. Like the traditional *schnorrer* da Costa does not beg. He impudently claims what he wants, as when he takes the wealthy Grobstock's charity, his cast-off clothes, some new ones, a trunk to transport the clothes, and a footman to transport the trunk.

Da Costa's success does not arise only from religious precept, from helping fellow Jews to be charitable. Da Costa relies on his style, which is his knowledge of Judaism. Da Costa believes he is forbidden to work to earn his money, and he proves his point using the Jewish law against work on the Sabbath. Da Costa is allowed only to pursue his sacred calling, as he tells Yankelé, his daughter's suitor, "*schnorring* and work should never be mixed" because "it brings temptation to work on the Sabbath."[10] Moreover, he asserts, "*schnorring* is the only occupation regular all the year round" (71). Da Costa's method is to visit the rich "in their own home [and not to lose] contact with the very people to whom you give the good deeds [of distributing charity]" (72). By making religion his style, da Costa achieves exactly what he wants and leaves his patrons gasping, aware they have given more than they intended but not sure by what means the extortion took place. Da Costa forces the bewildered Grobstock to invite him to Sabbath dinner, to which the *schnorrer* himself invites Yankelé as his own guest and treats Yankelé as if Grobstock's home were his own. When he *schnorrs* from the foppish Beau Belasco, da Costa quickly becomes the arbiter of the young dandy's clothing style, taking most of Belasco's new wardrobe for the poor, borrowing his carriage to transport the clothes, and receiving Belasco's feeble thanks.

Da Costa achieves his crowning success, lifetime support, through his knowledge of Judaism. When the Ashkenazic Yankelé wins da Costa's daughter by *schnorring* better than his mentor, the governing board of the Sephardic synagogue summons da Costa. The board refuses to allow members of the two Jewish groups to marry and threatens to excommunicate the beggar. Manasseh demolishes the board's arguments against the marriage by demonstrating that the rule by which they would prevent the union does not actually exist. In addition, he argues that as a beggar he, rather than any of the wealthy Jews, is a pillar of the synagogue and the community because he cements both through charity. Finally, da Costa has himself installed as King of the *schnorrers* on the basis of his knowledge. On the Sabbath preceding the marriage, da Costa pledges £100—money he does not have—to the synagogue for charity. By personal visits he raises two-thirds of the sum, on the strength of his assertion that the synagogue made a bad debt. Forcing Grobstock to invest the money because "the service of the Almighty demands the best men. I was the best man to collect the money—you are the best to invest it" (155), da Costa makes £600. He first pays his pledge. With the remaining £500, he sets up in the synagogue the da Costa fund, a life annuity for a "poor and deserving member of the congregation" (156)—himself. Zangwill ingeniously demonstrates that it is the man of learning, the one who uses his wits as well as his Jewish knowledge to work within Judaism, who succeeds. That similar situations did not frequently occur, Zangwill attests. Most of his fiction depicts Jews who chafe against what they perceive as the restrictive coils of Judaism. For them knowledge comes slowly and bitterly or their fund of Jewish knowledge fails to bring personal happiness.

Unlike Phillips and Frankau, indeed, unlike any of the other nineteenth-century Anglo-Jewish novelists, Zangwill expresses and embodies the Jewish tradition of argument in his fiction. As he sums up the century in his short stories and novels, he portrays the intellectual division within his religion at the close of Victoria's reign. On the one hand he depicts the old ways of the ghetto, which hemmed in Jews with hard but clear restrictions that nonetheless simultaneously buoyed them up with centuries-old truth revealed in Mosaic law and given to the world; as one character says, "We are a people that build for others" (*Ghetto Tragedies*, 121). On the other hand he portrays the gleam of the new world with its more liberal ways, which could free some Jews to live as they might have fantasized—to mingle easily with Christians, to lose many of the restrictions—in reality as having too much freedom to make any comfortable choice. Incorporating the three challenges faced by Anglo-Jewish novelists during the century, Zangwill transcends these themes as he questions the very nature of Judaism. At the same time he is more artistically successful because he presents a lucid, sociologically accurate, and frequently moving picture of young people struggling to grow as individuals and Jews while they grapple with parental and religious problems. His vision of coming generations of Jews and the future of Judaism is at once more sympathetic and more far-sighted, granting possibilities neither suggested nor explored by the other Anglo-Jewish novelists. Better known than them, Zangwill deserves his acceptance as the best.

CHAPTER 7

Conclusion

W E have thus far examined the fifteen Anglo-Jewish novelists'
responses to three challenges of the nineteenth century. Together, the novels under consideration portray what it meant to be a
nineteenth-century Jew. The major occurrences which form nineteenth-century Anglo-Jewish history and consume much of the
novels' attention are responses to English society and acculturation
to English life; the impact on the community made by life in
England is confirmed by historical data of the period. The subjects
of anti-Semitism, conversion, assimilation, intermarriage, and immigration partially indicate the nature of the social and religious
agitation within the community. In turn, the novels depict the
agitation.

The novels we have examined reflect a concomitant change in
narrative attitude. Only two of fifteen novelists plead for tolerance of
Jews; in contrast, the later writers seem to address a religiously
mixed audience without anticipating rejection by their English
readers. Equally important, the impact of acculturation manifests
itself in decreased description—distanced as it is—of traditional
Jewish rituals, festivals, and customs along with increased description of contemporary changes in religious adherence.

All the novelists may not have intended primarily to instruct the
non-Jewish reader by including this Jewish lore. Its presence does
suggest, at the very least, that the novelists were becoming accultured. Early authors probably distanced Judaism for fear of offending
their English audience, whereas later novelists presented Judaism to
lament the move away from Orthodoxy. In their fiction Anglo-
Jewish novelists are influenced by their contemporary situation, by
forces outside of Judaism which have an impact on the Jewish
community, and by Orthodox Jewish practice.

The Anglo-Jewish novelists' conscious response to their heritage provides a rhetoric that simultaneously engaged their Jewish audience and educated their English audience. The tradition they shared with fellow Jews allowed novelists and readers a particularly intimate form of communication. The novelists' attitude toward conversion is one example which reveals this unique kind of communication. Throughout the seventy-year period which begins with the Moss sisters and ends with Israel Zangwill, conversion receives narrative, communal, and religious disapproval. Moreover, even within the area of religious accommodation—the changing attitude toward intermarriage, for example—Anglo-Jewish novelists faithfully reflect a less traditional but equally real communality: the general attitude of the Anglo-Jewish community as regards intermarriage changed markedly, from disapproval to acquiescence, during the nineteenth century. English readers not familiar with Judaism would not participate in the special communication shared by Jewish novelists and readers. Nevertheless, these readers of Anglo-Jewish fiction did learn more about Jews and Judaism.

Anglo-Jewish novelists' response to their heritage is not the only sociological element molding their rhetoric. They were familiar with the image of the Jew in the novels written by non-Jewish Victorians as well. Whether Anglo-Jewish novelists show the humanity beneath the stereotype or offer an alternative, their response, particularly to the negative image, is a significant element in the rhetoric of Anglo-Jewish fiction.

Furthermore, Anglo-Jewish novels may well have influenced Victorian novelists. Two examples of notorious Jewish characters, one from each end of the period, illustrate the change in the English characterization of the figure of the Jew. The early example, Fagin (Dickens, *Oliver Twist*, 1838), is constructed according to the conventional negative stereotype. Although the later one, Svengali (Du Maurier, *Trilby*, 1894), might seem yet another product of that conventional view, there are major differences which indicate a modification of it, such that even an evil Jew is portrayed as a complex human being with not just inherent vices but needs and virtues.[1] To compare Fagin and Svengali is to understand in a broader and deeper way the context out of which Anglo-Jewish novelists wrote and the effect on the English characters their works had by 1894. Both are evil men, related to Judaism only by the name Jew, but they are linked indissolubly with all Jews. Most probably neither Dickens nor Du Maurier was knowingly anti-Semitic. Yet their portraits of Fagin and Svengali show simultaneously the similarity and the difference in the way Jews were perceived at the beginning and the end of the century by the English community.

Dickens's Fagin is a composite of Jews as they are represented in early dramas (see Chapter 1). He sports the red hair and whiskers of Judas and makes eloquent use of his eyebrows to help communicate his mood. As a fence, Fagin is worse than the early usurer, who worked within the law. While he has the craftiness of Marlowe's Barabas (*The Jew of Malta*), he is worse, a procurer and an assassin, informing on other underworld figures out of cupidity and to insure his own security, and even trying to use one person (Nancy) to eliminate another (Bill Sikes). Furthermore, at the end of the novel Fagin displays the cowardliness inherent in Shadrach Boaz (*The Young Quaker*). He does not speak with Shadrach's gibberish, possibly because Dickens wanted Fagin to be clearly understood and not comic. To have presented him as a comic figure would have been to work against his characterization as a representative of pervasive evil. Like Dryden's Sancho (*Love Triumphant*), Fagin is a nominal Jew—his only link to his religion is that others acknowledge him as "the Jew." Had he been characterized as a believer in God, Fagin would have been less credible as a soulless, inhuman criminal.

Not only does Fagin embody the Western myth of the criminal and mercantile Jew. He is also directly linked to the devil. Like his legendary counterpart, Fagin's origins are unknown. No one even speculates upon them. The bearded alien seems to have materialized in the London underworld where a soulless man could find temporary sanctuary and success. Other associations as well bind Fagin to Satan: his residence, his restriction to night travel, his physical appearance, and his Satanic powers. Fagin's residence is a refuge against the hostility of the outside world.[2] Variously called a "den" (186, 244) and a "lair" (416), it is not snug like an animal's nest but dirty, gloomy, and diabolically subterranean. From his den Fagin emerges only at night and, like the devil, leaves no footprints; he moves like a "loathsome reptile, engendered in the slime and darkness" (186). In addition, Fagin closely resembles Satan. His few teeth are "fangs as should have been a dog's or a rat's," and he looks like "some hideous phantom, moist from the grave" (417). Other characters recognize the relationship between Fagin and the devil. The narrator calls Fagin "the merry old gentleman" (110), an appellation which commonly refers to Satan. Sikes looks at Fagin's "withered old claw" and says, " 'Reminds me of being nabbed by the devil' " (398). Demonic power resides in Fagin's ability to change the appearance of others for his own benefit and in his disappearance from the Maylie's: "The search was all in vain. There were not even the traces of recent footsteps, to be seen" (32).

Dickens underscores Fagin's malevolence and his Satanic power by continued descriptive reference to his facial expression. There is ample English and Continental literary tradition for the Jew who punctuates vocal and physical expression with pronounced gesticulation, but Dickens reduces this grotesque aspect to a focus upon Fagin's facial expressiveness. Fagin uses his eyebrows instead of bodily gestures. But his most impressive organs of communication, in frequency and in quality of description, are his eyes. The precedent for the power and effect of the Jewish gaze extends back through Matthew Lewis and Maria Edgeworth to the legend of the Wandering Jew. While Fagin's is not the enthralling evil eye, used for example by Lewis in *The Monk,* his glance is frightening enough to make the vicious Bill Sikes exclaim, " 'D——— your eyes!' " (188).

Fagin is unlike the legendary Wandering Jew in two ways, neither of which represents a move toward a positive depiction. First, Fagin's spellbinding gaze ultimately fails. Oliver does not become a thief; Nancy will not murder Sikes; and Sikes disregards Fagin's plea that he be " 'not too violent for safety' " (421), a disregard that leads circuitously, but finally, to Fagin's capture. Second, instead of wandering until his soul is redeemed, Fagin dies without salvation. The rabbis who come to pray with him are "driven away with curses" (469). Here, however, Dickens may well have claimed deliberately *not* to be anti-Semitic. Fagin's rejection of the rabbis directly suggests that Fagin is a nominal Jew (as, of course, are virtually all negatively portrayed Jews in English literature), and not a religious, Orthodox Jew. Jewish readers could recognize Fagin's nominal adherence to his religion and castigate him, as Anglo-Jewish novelists denigrate nominal Jews in the novels we have examined. From the viewpoint of Anglo-Jewish novelists who portray nominal Jews as evil, Fagin's irreligion may make him a more evil but, paradoxically, a less anti-Semitic character. For the Christian reader, however, the distinction is not so clear. That Fagin is called "the Jew" and that his religious affiliation is tied to his evil nature is enough to link Fagin with negative feelings about all Jews.[3]

Fagin thus embodies the tradition of the negatively stereotyped Jew in history and literature. In addition, Dickens expands Fagin's capacity for evil in two ways: as the gang-master and as a predator on the innocent. As the controlling force and guardian of the gang, Fagin teaches the boys how to steal and disciplines them with blows, all for his own gain. He is a perverse kind of schoolmaster recognizable to any Victorian. Clearly beneath the schoolmaster image lurks, however, the image of Fagin as Satan, directing his minions to do his work and to seduce new members into the gang. In a far more rapacious manner he preys on the innocent. Fagin corrupted Nancy when a child, and he tries to reproduce in Oliver the success he achieved with Nancy: he uses the knowledge of past crimes to coerce the victim into performing further crimes. Like a snake, Fagin first injects the venom of crime into his victim and then slowly steals his victim's soul with each additional crime. A description of Fagin's conditioning process as used on Oliver delineates this very process while suggesting that Fagin is a snake: "The wily old Jew had the boy in his toils. . . . He was now slowly instilling into his soul the poison which he hoped would blacken it . . . for ever" (185). The image of Fagin as a snake ties him even more closely to traditional Evil.

If Fagin's demonic qualities make him an unsympathetic character, his success in corrupting Nancy and his attempt to steal Oliver's soul position Fagin for the role of scapegoat at his trial. In court, "all looks were fixed upon one man—the Jew. . . . But in no one face . . . could Fagin read the faintest sympathy with himself, or any feeling but one of all-absorbing interest that he should be condemned" (466). As in the old ritual cleansing there is nothing personal in the sacrifice of Fagin. He is merely the symbol of society's guilt; as such he must be removed. Thus, when the jury returns with the verdict of guilty, it is met with "a peal of joy from the populace outside, greeting the news that he would die on Monday" (468).

Dickens and his English readers, no less than Anglo-Jewish novelists and their Jewish readers, shared the nineteenth-century tradition of middle-class morality which, in addition to involving various common prejudices and misconceptions, demands that justice be done, that anyone who sins must be punished. This concept would seem to be the middle-class individual's way of retaining the orderly surface of society, so that he may complacently ignore the troubled depths. Moreover, responsibility for the trouble in the depths must paradoxically be both unacknowledged and transferred to a scapegoat. In *Oliver Twist* blame for society's vices is relegated to a villainous Jewish scapegoat.

The thrust of Victorian morality was, in part, a rigid dedication to a strict sense of the "right" and the "good." Only limited extenuation and tolerance for deviations from established standards were permitted. Among the heathen aborigines of the expanding Colonial empire, for example, temporary aberrations might be allowed with the knowledge that the Church and the government had created a timetable for correction. Similarly, Bill Sikes could be forgiven for his sinful existence because of his almost aboriginal existence, because of his moral seduction by Fagin, and even because of the absence of a kindly vicar. But who is Fagin's Fagin? Could Fagin be considered even remotely ignorant? And, had the Church taken an interest in him, would Fagin have responded? Dickens's silence leads the reader to infer that Fagin is intrinsically and irrevocably evil, is possessed of demonic intelligence, and has no interest in redemption to the last. The Victorian reader, repelled by the total absence of any redeeming personal quality in Fagin, condemned the Jew as an embodiment of absolute evil. This intense feeling of righteousness allowed the final emotional thrust: by making Fagin a scapegoat, the middle-class reader's loyalty to morality could be discharged at the same time that he or she, as a citizen, could ignore the actual conditions of all the Bill Sikeses and Nancys in England. Like the courtroom spectators, the reader could be joyous over Fagin's end, vicariously realizing the desire for justice, potentially dangerous here because this desire is fulfilled by the death of the Jew.

The intense feeling against Fagin-the-demon is inseparable from his ethnic identity which, in the text, continuously reinforces his malevolence. The end result is not simply a scapegoat but a Jewish scapegoat, with anti-Semitism superimposed on and justified by the fight against evil. Even the most liberal Victorian reader, who claimed not to be anti-Semitic, could not help but react against Fagin. There is no need to doublecheck one's reactions, to sympathize momentarily with Fagin, to pause to extenuate any of his actions. Dickens has unerringly led his audience, backed by their monolithic, Victorian sense of justice and righteousness, to anti-Semitism through a morally abominable character, conveniently and simultaneously Jewish. Dickens's Victorian concern for morality seems thus to have combined with an inherited anti-Semitic rhetoric to produce yet another negative stereotype of a Jew, already so familiar to his readers.

The character of Svengali likewise arises from the traditional negative stereotype of the Jew. Like Fagin, Svengali is "dirty" and "sinister" (11); he has a devilish leer "that was not engaging" (29). Like Shadrach Boaz and Fagin, he is a coward, "always ready to vex, frighten, bully, torment anybody or anything smaller and weaker than himself" (114). Du Maurier does not make explicit the relationship between Svengali and Satan, although his leer, his sinister appearance, "canine" teeth (136), and that he seems to be "a dread, powerful demon . . . an incubus" (136–37) suggest their bond. Du Maurier does tie his villain to the Wandering Jew, a link forged by Svengali's enthralling evil eye, his roaming the earth, and his mesmerizing powers. The power and success of Svengali's malevolent glance is more directly related to the Wandering Jew of Monk Lewis's novel than to Fagin.

In yet other ways, Du Maurier's villainous Jew is different from Dickens's. The stereotype of the late nineteenth century included the Jew as social invader, the insensitive boor who lacked the breeding to fit into genteel society but who continually tried. Svengali is not only physically repulsive, his personality is equally repugnant. His humor is "cynical" and "offensive," for he "always laughed at the wrong thing, at the wrong time, in the wrong place. And his laughter was always derisive and full of malice. And his egotism and conceit were not to be borne" (57). His playfulness is sinister and feline: "When he cringed, it was with a mock humility full of sardonic threats; when he was playful, it was with a terrible playfulness, like that of a cat with a mouse—a weird ungainly cat, and most unclean" (108). His voice is associated with the carrion-eating rook, and his expression while speaking is equally beastly and alien:

these vicious imaginations of Svengali's, which look so tame in English print, sounded much more ghastly in French, pronounced with a Hebrew-German accent, and uttered in his hoarse, rasping, nasal, throaty rook's caw, his big yellow teeth baring themselves in a mongrel canine snarl, his heavy upper eyelids drooping over his insolent black eyes. (136)

In sum he is "about as bad as they make 'em" (59). But Svengali's sinister qualities are undercut by his foreign accent. Svengali's language bears the mark of Shadrach Boaz's gibberish. He speaks nasal, broken English throughout the novel. While comic effect would have destroyed Fagin's malevolence and made moralization difficult, Svengali's jargon enables the reader to share the narrator's contempt for and mockery of Svengali, the immigrant Jew.

Whereas Dickens's villainous Jew looks back to past figures, Du Maurier's portrait embraces more contemporary characteristics. For example, Svengali's accomplished yet magical musicianship adds one modern facet to Du Maurier's depiction of the Jew: by the end of the nineteenth century, the European Jews, especially those in Eastern Europe, had established a well-deserved reputation for musical talent. Entertainment was one of the few fields of professional endeavor open to Jewish participation—and Svengali is "only to be endured for the sake of his music" (114).

Du Maurier adds another new twist to anti-Semitic portraits with the character of Svengali. The novelist applies the principle of homeopathic medicine, then in vogue, to popular prejudice against the late nineteenth-century waves of Jewish immigrants. By showing that what is good in small doses is irremediably evil in large doses, Du Maurier presents anti-Semitism obliquely through compliment. Consider the description of Little Billee, the sentimental hero. Little Billee has an "infinitesimal dose of the good old Oriental blood" (236) to keep him morally correct. The evidence of that inheritance is present in his face:

just a faint suggestion of some possibly very remote Jewish ancestor—just a tinge of that strong, sturdy, irrepressible, indomitable, indelible blood which is of such priceless value in diluted homeopathic doses. . . . Fortunately for the world, and especially for ourselves, most of us have in our veins at least a minim of that precious fluid, whether we know it or not. *Tant pis pour les autres!* (6—7)

The difference between Little Billee's desirable drop of Jewish blood and Svengali's villainous, undiluted share constitutes anti-Semitism. The poison, strychnine, becomes in small doses the tonic, strychnine; the diseased full-blooded Jew, when infinitely diluted, becomes the noble Victorian Englishman. Svengali is the poison, Little Billie the tonic. The alien Jew could not be accepted as he was. To some English minds, a full-blooded Jew, Svengali, is the same as a demon or viper. But a mere drop "of that precious fluid" in Little Billee's veins generates within him the proper morality. Du Maurier is not the only Englishman addressing himself to the subject of the Jew to believe that Englishmen are fortunate to possess a "tinge" of Jewish blood. Toward the end of his sociological study, Charles Russell states, "Whatever may be thought of the Jewish character in itself, there is no doubt that an infusion of Jewish blood would introduce an admirable strain into the breed of Englishmen" (*The Jew in London*, 138).

Despite the carefully wrought description of Svengali, he is never dramatically viewed acting evilly toward Trilby. The only scene of actual mesmerism occurs when Svengali removes the pain of a simple headache. When he is presented dramatically, Svengali merely frightens Trilby because she will not love him. Svengali, the alien Jew, mesmerizes Trilby for his own gain, and she sins by living with the already married pianist whom she treats "with the obedience of a dog" (372). But because Trilby lacks control over herself when she is hypnotized, in intent she remains morally pure. Svengali's use of the occult, in the form of mesmerism, is thus sexually titallating, despite the fact that neither occult machinations nor sex appear dramatically in the text. The implicit suggestion in Trilby's lack of will and in her wasting away of a "physical weakness" (401) after Svengali dies is that Trilby's soul has been stolen. This suggestion becomes explicit when, with a further reinforcement of Svengali's villainy, a picture of the mesmerist is delivered from "the poisonous East—birthplace and home of an ill wind that blows nobody good" (432) to Trilby on her deathbed. She gazes at the photograph, sings angelically as she has when mesmerized by Svengali, and dies. Arriving immediately thereafter and unaware of what has just transpired, the doctor tells her friends that she has been dead for "perhaps a quarter of an hour" (435). Svengali's potent evil strikes from beyond the grave, the implication being that he is in league with the devil.

Unlike Fagin, Svengali does not become a classic scapegoat. He dies not from legal persecution but of a heart attack, presumably induced by the taunts of his rival, Little Billee, and Little Billee's friends. The anti-Semitism directed toward Svengali is, however, more directly anti-Jewish than the anti-Semitism directed toward Fagin, which is secondary to the evil Fagin symbolizes. Svengali is an alien and is regarded as an inferior; he is treated contemptuously by his English friends and by the narrator and "deserves" this treatment because he is a Jew.

Consider the following as an example of overt anti-Semitism in *Trilby*: Svengali spits at his rival, causing a fight. Afterwards, one of Little Billee's friends reflects, "He had, for hours, the feel of that long, thick, shapely Hebrew nose being kneaded between his gloved knuckles, and a pleasing sense of the effectiveness of the tweak he had given it" (364). Other characters think similarly. The shape of one man's nose is linked to those of all others of his religion and recalls in yet another way Svengali's Jewishness and, for some readers, anti-Semitic emotions. Furthermore, the narrator explicitly ties Svengali's religion, highlighted by four adjectives, to the pianist's desire to humiliate, if not murder, Little Billee: "being an *Oriental Israelite Hebrew Jew*, Svengali had not been able to resist the temptation of spitting in his face, since he must not throttle him to death" (370, emphasis mine). The Englishmen treat Svengali contemptuously each time they encounter him until Svengali finally dies as a result of their taunts. Portrayed differently from Fagin, Svengali is nonetheless an outcast and an alien, and he dies rejected by an English society of which he is never a part.

Like Dickens, Du Maurier creates a stereotyped Jewish villain. Du Maurier's depiction of Svengali resonates, however, less with traditional anti-Semitism than with contemporary characteristics of the Jew as a sinister yet comic figure. The suggestion of Svengali's debasement of Trilby arouses the reader's horror no less than Fagin's degradation of his gang members. The reader recoils from Svengali when, to achieve his own worldly success, he saps Trilby's moral strength, mesmerizing her "with one look of his eye" (458) and the command, *"Et maintenant dors, ma mignonne"* (394). The synthesis of traditional and contemporary anti-Semitic characteristics in the figure of Svengali, compared with Fagin, indicates the change in the Victorian image of the Jew—Svengali is not capable of arousing the fear that Fagin does—and simultaneously the unchanging denigration implicit in that image—for all the laughter heaped upon Svengali, he does steal Trilby's soul.

Although Fagin and Svengali, the most powerful figures in their respective novels, are invested with pervasive evil, Svengali is far tamer, possessing a smaller power base and so affecting fewer people. This softening of the late Victorian image of the Jew indicates that Anglo-Jewish novelists elicited some acceptance for their people. Reading Anglo-Jewish fiction in the context of the evolving perspective implied by Victorian fiction thus points not only to the changing position of the Jew in English society, but also in the English mind; even as Anglo-Jewish fiction directly or indirectly responded to the negative English stereotyping of the Jew, it influenced these stereotypes.

Study of the parallel between the way Anglo-Jews reacted to non-Jewish portraits of them and at the same time saw themselves in their own fiction reveals not only how their works refract life but also that social life and literature mix significantly. In meeting the challenges of anti-Semitism and the conversionists, Anglo-Jewish novelists successfully portrayed strong and clear role models for positive Jewish behavior. In warning against acculturation, intermarriage, and assimilation, and in dealing with the immigrant, they were not triumphant. Acculturation for not a few led to intermarriage and assimilation. Some later novelists approve even of intermarriage, an attitude which reflects awareness of some Jews' assimilation to English society as well as these novelists' own acculturation. While warning Jews of the religious upheaval the novelists saw besetting and undermining their community, they view the upward social movement of fellow Jews keenly and critically. They harshly criticize the nominal Jew as an evil in their midst and disdain the materialistic Jew, unfailingly positing the failure in his personal life. Finally, they lament and warn against the move away from Orthodoxy by predicting that more Jews of the next generation will assimilate. Five novelists, Meritor, Harris, Sidgwick, Levy, and Frankau, see Orthodoxy ultimately losing its already tenuous hold on the community and nominal Judaism or assimilation replacing it. Farjeon suggests that some Jews will remain Orthodox and others will assimilate. Zangwill, the sole novelist to postulate Zionism as a possible solution, is pessimistic about the success of a Jewish homeland. Instead, he proffers Orthodoxy or Reform Judaism as viable choices for the future and condemns assimilation. Only Gordon continuously believes Orthodoxy will dominate.

Twentieth-century Anglo-Jews travel all paths projected by the novelists. In the Jewish community while converts are more readily accepted and acculturation is an individual choice—as predicted by Zangwill—the nominal Jew continues to be an evil, insofar as he removes himself and his family from Judaism and helps to shrink from within the community the number of practicing Jews, and the materialistic Jew still receives disdain. Fear of the disappearance of Judaism through intermarriage or assimilation grows, not just in Jewish communities in England but all over the world. Despite their projections for the future, Anglo-Jewish novelists do not offer a fictional vision very different from the contemporary reality of the community.

Individual Anglo-Jewish novels do not offer the kind of vision found in the "great" works of the Victorian period. Most characters fit a Procrustean bed and fail to do more than embody a thinly disguised point. Anglo-Jewish novelists, as representatives of a minority culture sporadically under attack but in an improving and liberating situation, responded to English stereotypes of the Jew and thus tended themselves to stereotype, not infrequently attributing exaggerated virtue to Jews. As external conditions improved, the novelists tended to write to other Jews, urging them to "keep the faith," setting a pattern frequently followed by writers of other minority groups. Nineteenth-century Anglo-Jewish novelists who chose to write about Jews presented stereotyped Jews, dilemmas with which the community struggled, attitudes that changed during the century, and projections for the future of Judaism; together they provide a social history of Victorian Anglo-Jews that vividly depicts problems of this minority group as it became freed from political and social restrictions.

Notes and References

Preface

1. Israel Zangwill, *The Voice of Jerusalem* (London: Heinemann, 1920), p. 201.

2. Zangwill, *Children of the Ghetto; A Study of a Peculiar People* (New York: Macmillan, 1898), p. 329. Subsequent references are to this edition and are cited in the text.

Chapter One

1. According to Joshua Tractenberg, *The Devil and the Jew: The Medieval Conception of the Jew and Its Relation to Modern Anti-Semitism* (New Haven: Yale University Press, 1943), the theological and the popular basis of anti-Semitism rests on the belief that Jews killed Christ. In addition, Christians who interpreted the Old Testament as prophesying the coming of Jesus could not comprehend the Jews' rejection of the Messiah. Since there could be no question in Christian theology that Jesus Christ was the Messiah, the only logical conclusions were that Jews were ignorant or perverse. Intermittently until the tenth century, official Church policy preached tolerance in the hope that Jews would realize their error and convert. When few converted, the Jews' status was reappraised, and they were reclassified as less than human. It was only a step further to connect the Jews with the Devil, the ultimate anti-Christ. Structured by official Church policy, this relationship of the two enemies of Christendom filtered down to the already hostile and superstitious masses as undeniable truth. Thus, while socioeconomic reasons appear prominent in persecutions of Jews, the religious basis of anti-Semitic prejudice that morally supports such persecution must be remembered.

Kenneth N. Gould, *They Got the Blame: The Story of Scapegoats in History* (New York: Association Press, 1942), pp. 9−34, shows that another, perhaps subconscious, basis of popular anti-Semitism lies in the transference of blame for society's ills to any available scapegoat. Responsibility thus placed permits a society to cleanse itself of guilt for those ills and simultaneously to ignore the real problem which created that guilt. One common abuse of the scapegoat phenomenon was that it provided the existing power structure with the opportunity to persecute an individual or a minority group at times of extreme pressure to remove attention from social or political failures. In this manner the Jew has been a scapegoat of Western society. Proscribed from owning land by the Church after A.D. 70, he became either a moneylender or a merchant because money was the easiest of goods to smuggle in times of persecution. When the Church forbade usury to its members, the Jew, under the Crown's protection in most European countries, fulfilled the function of banker for the Middle Ages. In this position the Jew received the hostility of those who were in debt to him and ultimately, in the way he was expelled from England and from Spain two centuries later, became a scapegoat.

Folk legend, too, played its part in creating public hostility against the Jew, according to Joseph Gaer, *The Legend of the Wandering Jew* (New York: Mentor, 1961), pp. 1−45. The masses saw the Jew, who was conspicuous in his environment, as an alien and inferior figure. Even if the Jew adapted himself to his environment, even if he surrendered his identity or converted, he remained a Jew to others, a distinction which earned him second class rights, if any. Moreover, the myth of the Jew as sorcerer was generally accepted as truth. A fantasy built on superstition and reinforced by propaganda, it perniciously entrenched itself as the myth of the Wandering Jew, which pictured the Jew as eternally rootless, searching for his soul and redemption. In the fifteenth century he was to acquire the attributes of spellbinder and evil magician. Many during the Middle Ages believed that the Jew guarded fabulous treasure; they also ascribed to the Jew possession of the evil eye, a foul odor (*foetor judaicus*) composed of sulphur and brimstone, arising from his connection with Satan, and the power to afflict Christians with the loss of blood, a necessary ingredient in his sorcery. During times of sociopolitical crisis it was convenient to invoke this myth against the Jew.

2. The discussion of Anglo-Jewish history in this chapter is indebted to Albert Montefiore Hyamson, *A History of the Jews in England*, 2nd ed. (London: Metheun, 1928), and Cecil Roth, *A History of the Jews in England* (London: Oxford University Press, 1941).

3. The origin of the word Sephardic is rooted in the biblical Hebrew referent for Spain. Until the late fifteenth century Jews migrated from Spain and Portugal to France and Germany and thence to Central and Eastern Europe. During the 1490s practicing Jews were totally expelled from the Iberian peninsula. They set up homogeneous communities in Europe, North Africa, and the Near East, distinct from their brethren of earlier migrations who had by then partially assimilated. A small fraction were permitted to remain in Spain and Portugal, contingent upon their conversion to Catholicism. A smaller number continued to practice Judaism secretly while pretending Catholicism in public. These secret Jews were known as Marranos. Those who were expelled and their descendants are known today, regardless of their nationality, as Sephardim; but in common

usage and in this study the term will be directed to those émigrés who settled in Western Europe, particularly Holland after the expulsion.

Jewish communities in Western Europe beyond Spain and Portugal existed during the Roman Empire. They began to have distinctive cultural and spiritual characteristics after the breakdown of communications which followed the Roman Empire's political disintegration during the fifth century A.D. These communities were augmented intermittently by settlers from Spain and Portugal during the Middle Ages. Their population growth, periodic persecution, and greater economic and political freedom in Eastern and Central Europe catalyzed large-scale movements of Jews toward the East until the seventeenth century. The elimination of the more Moorish-oriented Sephardic communities west of the Pyrenees in the fifteenth century and the resultant cultural isolation of the balance of European Jews further insured their unique and separate ethnic evolution. This group, varying somewhat from boundary to boundary in custom and speech, is called Ashkenazim to differentiate them from the equally distinct Sephardim.

The essential differences between the Sephardim and the Ashkenazim lie in their class consciousness, liturgy, interpretation of the Bible, and pronunciation of Hebrew (although since the State of Israel was established in 1948, Jews have increasingly adopted Sephardic pronunciation, following Israel's lead). The widely traveled cosmopolitan Sephardim, always clannish, accentuated their differences and their sense of separatism when in contact with their Ashkenazic brethren. As the first Jews in England in the seventeenth century, they looked down upon the Ashkenazim, to whom they were economically and socially superior. Because they were international bankers and mercantile traders, the Sephardim were thrown into early, easy contact with the English aristocracy and became acculturated. When the Ashkenazim arrived in England their majority belonged to the servant class or were small traders and peddlers. They dressed poorly and moved only within their own narrow circle. They embarrassed the Sephardim, who declined to be classed with Jews commonly insulted by the English populace and with whom they were linked only by religion. (The Ashkenazim reacted similarly in the late nineteenth century when waves of new Ashkenazic immigrants reached England. The acculturated Ashkenazim solved their embarrassment by settling most of the immigrants outside London.) Marriage between an Ashkenazi and a Sephardi was frowned upon; the Sephardic synagogue did not recognize such a marriage until 1706, although members of each community intermarried previous to that year. The two groups of Jews, separated since the early days of Christianity, remain separate communities in England.

Cecil Roth, *A History of the Marranos* (Philadelphia: Jewish Publication Society of America, 1947); Albert M. Hyamson, *The Sephardim of England: A History of the Spanish and Portuguese Jewish Community, 1492–1951* (London: Metheun, 1951).

4. Hyamson, A *History of the Jews,* p. 141.

5. Hyamson, p. 243; B. R. Mitchell and Phyllis Deane, *Abstract of British Historical Statistics* (Cambridge, England: University Press, 1962), p. 8. Subsequent statistics concerning Jews are from Hyamson, concerning England from Mitchell and Deane. All statistics from Mitchell and Deane, referring to the population of England, include the populations of England and Wales.

6. For detailed discussions of trades Jews entered see Z. D. Litman, *A Social History of the Jews in England: 1850—1950* (London: Watts, 1954), pp. 27—30, who states that by 1840 there was a sharp decline of Jewish street vendors because an influx of poor Irish immigrants took over; because Jews, restricted to being wholesale merchants until the end of the seventeenth century, had by then made some money peddling and turned to a trade; because Jewish youngsters by then were apprenticed to trades such as tailoring and cabinetry; and because Jewish interest in clothing, dating from when Jews were secondhand traders, developed into an interest in tailoring and retailing.

7. V. D. Lipman, "The Age of Emancipation: 1815-1880," *Three Centuries of Anglo-Jewish History,* ed. V. D. Lipman (Cambridge, England: The Jewish Historical Society of England, 1961), p. 74, notes that this ratio differs from that of the general population in which the lower class predominated.

8. Lipman, *Social History,* pp. 50—57.

9. M. Dorothy George, *London Life in the Eighteenth Century* (New York: Knopf, 1925), pp. 125—34. Jewish political and civil disabilities would be removed only gradually, each step attended by the resumption of superstition and hostility.

10. Cecil Roth, *A History of the Jews,* p. 233.

11. For a detailed discussion of emigration during the latter decades of the nineteenth century see Lloyd P. Gartner, *The Jewish Immigrant in England, 1870—1914* (London: George Allen and Unwin, 1960).

12. Despite Rothschild's loyalty to the English Crown, in 1830 he was satirized as a greedy financier. The following poem was reprinted in *The Atheneum; or, Spirit of the English Magazines* ser. 3, 4 (1830), 238:

> I'd be a Rothschild! immortal in story,
>> As the fellows who live by their stanzas and brains:
> Having a heart drunk with visions of glory,
>> When fifty percent. on my table remains.
> I'd have no poet to sway his lute o'er me,
>> A fig for the head that such nonsense contains:
> I'd be a Rothschild, immortal in story,
>> As the fellows who live by their stanzas and brains.
>
> Tell me of Southies and Scotts—they are ninnies
>> To foolishly trifle with time as they do;
> Give me the music of soul-witching Guineas

While they address lays to the "summer skies blue."
What if they scribble like Virgils and Plinies,
   At sixpence per line in each London review?
I'd be a Rothschild! and laugh at such ninnies,
   Whose brains such absurd undertakings pursue.

Commerce shall wave her proud flag o'er the ocean,
   When the wreath and the minstrel have vanish'd from hence;
Rhymes may give to the muse their devotion,
   But *mine* is concentred in consols and rents.
Of Tempé and Castaly I have no notion,
   Oh, they give song the importance of sense;
I'd be a Rothschild! with every emotion
   Awake to tune of *pounds, shillings* and *pence.*

13. This portion of Anglo-Jewish history is indebted to Hyamson; Lipman, *Social History* and *Three Centuries;* and Sidney Salomon, *The Jews of Britain* (London: Jarrolds, 1938).

14. Evangelical sects emphasized returning to the basic tenets of Christianity, spreading their faith, and concentrating on the individual's relationship to God at the same time they deemphasized organized ritual.

15. Susan S. Tamke, *Make A Joyful Noise Unto the Lord: Hymns as A Reflection of Victorian Social Attitudes* (Athens, Ohio: Ohio University Press, 1978), p. 133. Subsequent references are cited in the text.

The religious revival which swept Europe and England during the early decades of the nineteenth century and which was to be a shaping influence of the Victorian period was assisted by religious novels and propaganda tracts. The religious novel began its lengthy and popular career during the 1830s. Its history extends back at least to Bunyan's *Pilgrim's Progress* (1678), but it emerged as a major force in the service of religion only in the nineteenth century. In quantity one of the most massive genres of the century, religious novels illustrate sincere faith in Christianity and bear a sharply moral imprint. According to Margaret Maison, *The Victorian Vision: Studies in the Religious Novel* (New York: Sheed and Ward, 1961), especially Chapters 2 and 3, they range from romances about clerical life to spiritual biographies and confessions to thinly disguised propaganda tracts. One major type is the conversion novel, popular from the 1830s through the 1890s. Evangelicals, Tractarians, Broad Churchmen, and Catholics wrote of their own conversions hoping to stir others; while many addressed Christians, a substantial number worked for the conversion of the Jews.

16. Montagu Frank Modder, *The Jew in the Literature of England* (1939; rpt. New York: Meridian Books, 1960), pp. 132−37, 148−52.

Novels about Jewish culture appear to be a natural outgrowth of the religious novel and another massive, minor literary genre of the nineteenth century, the "local color" novel. The "local color" novel, burgeoning from the time of Walter Scott and Maria Edgeworth, emphasizes milieu, colloquial speech, and life peripheral to that of the dominant English culture. Even manifestly diverse types of fiction, including the historical novel, the Newgate novel, the neo-Gothic novel, the domestic novel, and the "silver fork" novel, reveal kinship to each other in their focus on what it was like to be different. Novels about Judaism thus seem to be neither a peculiar nor a new type.

17. This portion of Anglo-Jewish history is indebted to Lipman, *Three Centuries,* pp. 86–179, *Social History,* pp. 36–135; James Picciotto, *Sketches of Anglo-Jewish History* (London: Trubner, 1875), pp. 198–201, 364–66; and Roth, *A History of the Jews,* pp. 196–263. Subsequent references to Picciotto are cited in the text.

18. Cecil Roth, *A History of the Jews,* p. 224; Lipman, "The Age of Emancipation: 1815–1880," *Three Centuries,* pp. 70–106.

19. Lipman, *Social History,* pp. 36–37, states that in 1851 10 percent of the London Jewish community attended Sabbath services, "the attendance figures of a community at least partially assimilated."

20. In my identification of nineteenth-century Anglo-Jewish novelists, I was greatly assisted by Rabbi Edward N. Calisch, *The Jew in English Literature as Author and Subject* (Richmond, Virginia: Bell, 1909), pp. 209–65; Rebecca Schneider, *Bibliography of Jewish Life in the Fiction of America and England* (Albany, N.Y.: New York State Library School, 1916), pp. 1–32; Montagu Frank Modder, *The Jew,* pp. 412–26; Leo J. Henkin, "Problems and Digressions in the Victorian Novel (1860–1900)," *Bulletin of Bibliography* 10:5 (1944): 105–107.

21. For a detailed discussion see M. J. Landa, *The Jew in Drama* (New York: William Morrow, 1927).

22. Modder, *The Jew,* discusses stereotypes of the Jew beginning with their appearance in medieval ballads.

Chapter Two

1. Celia and Marian Moss, *The Romance of Jewish History,* 3 vols. (London: Saunders and Otley, 1840), Dedication. Subsequent references are to the second edition, published in 1843 by Miller and Field, and are cited in the text by the abbreviation *RJH.*

2. Grace Aguilar, "The Jews in England," *Essays and Miscellanies— Choice Cullings,* selected by Sarah Aguilar (Philadelphia: A. Hart, 1853), p. 272.

3. Celia and Marian Moss, *Tales of Jewish History,* 3 vols. (London: Miller and Field, 1843). Subsequent references are to this edition and are cited in the text by the abbreviation *TJH.* Celia Moss Levetus, *The King's Physician and Other Tales* (Birmingham, England: T. Hinton, 1865). Biographical information on the Mosses is from the *Encyclopedia Judaica* (Jerusalem: Macmillan, 1971), VI, col. 984.

4. Beth-Zion Lask Abrahams, "Grace Aguilar: A Centenary Tribute," *Transactions of the Jewish Historical Society of England* 16 (1952): 137–48. Subsequent references are cited in the text.

5. Grace Aguilar, *Records of Israel* (London: J. Mortimer, 1844), p. x.

6. Philip M. Weinberger, "The Social and Religious Thought of Grace Aguilar (1816–1847)," Diss. New York University 1970, p. 46. Subsequent references are cited in the text.

7. *Home Influence* and *Vale of Cedars*, Aguilar's most popular novels, contain biographical memoirs written by Sarah Aguilar who edited her daughter's works after 1847.

8. For a definition of Scott's practice in historical fiction, see Georg Lukács, *The Historical Novel* (London: Merlin Press, 1962), p. 19.

9. Grace Aguilar, *Women of Israel* (London: R. Groombridge, 1845), p. 310. Subsequent references are cited in the text.

10. Grace Aguilar, *The Vale of Cedars; or, the Martyr* (New York: D. Appleton, 1872), p. 145. Subsequent references are to this edition and are cited in the text. *Vale of Cedars* can serve as a paradigm of the Anglo-Jewish novel. Consequently, I analyze it at length to illustrate how the plea for tolerance didactically shapes the novel and to exemplify some stereotypes in these novels, thereby preventing extensive repetition of character analysis.

11. Aguilar's knowledge of English stereotypes of Jews allows her to play with these stereotypes. For one thing, the piercing gaze traditionally assigned by non-Jewish writers to the Wandering Jew belongs here to the Catholic Queen, Isabella.

12. Another example is Aguilar's handling of the Sabbath, the weekly twenty-four hours of rest and prayer for Jews which spans from sundown on Friday evening to the appearance of the first three stars Saturday evening and which is as important as the High Holy Days. She presents the Sabbath in its essence as a time "from which in general all earthly cares and thoughts were banished, giving place to tranquil and spiritual joy" (39). Despite her statement of the Jewish Sabbath's essential idea, it lacks detail which would give the non-Jewish reader knowledge about a family's particular closeness during this weekly observance, when they are commanded by Jewish law to eat, study, and sing together. Toward the novel's close "the Sabbath lamps were lighted" (246), but without mention of their dominant place in ushering in the Sabbath and demarcating this weekly celebration from the rest of the week.

13. Quoted by Hyamson, *The Sephardim*, pp. 17–18.

14. Grace Aguilar, *Sabbath Thoughts and Sacred Communings* (London: R. Groombridge, 1853), p. 3.

15. Compare the description of Marie's coloring with Scott's description in *Ivanhoe* (Border Edition, London: Nimmo, 1893), XVI, 49, 96, of the English Rowena, "her complexion was exquisitely fair," and the Jewish Rebecca, "her turban of yellow silk suited well with the darkness of her complexion."

16. *English Catalogue of Books*, comp. Sampson Low, I, 8; IV, 6; V, 15; VII, 19; *British Museum General Catalogue of Printed Books*, II, 752–54; *National Union Catalog Pre–1956 Imprints*, V, 349–54. References to the numbers of editions throughout this study are to the latter two works.

17. *The George Eliot Letters*, ed. Gordon S. Haight (New Haven: Yale University Press, 1955), VI, 301.

18. Mrs. Alfred Sidgwick, *Home Life in Germany* (New York: Chautauqua Press, 1908), p. 1.

19. One of the seven novels, *Isaac Eller's Money* (1889), also listed as *Isaac Eiler's Money*, is regrettably unobtainable. The only extant copy, held by the British Museum, was lost or destroyed during World War II.

20. Mrs. Andrew Dean, pseud. [Mrs. Alfred Sidgwick], *Lesser's Daughter* (London: T. Fisher Unwin, 1894), p. 18. Subsequent references are to this edition, apparently the only English edition, and are cited in the text.

21. Dean, *A Woman with a Future* (London: Frederick A. Stokes, 1895).

22. Mrs. Alfred Sidgwick, *The Devil's Cradle* (New York: W. J. Watt, 1918), p. 110. Subsequent references are to this edition, apparently the only American edition, and are cited in the text.

23. Sidgwick, *Iron Cousins* (New York: W. J. Watt, 1919), pp. 60, 30. Subsequent references are to this edition, apparently the only American edition, and are cited in the text. The employer also disparages a Jewish family as "those rich Jews" (87), recalling medieval English anti-Semitism.

24. Sidgwick, *Refugee* (London: Collins, 1934), pp. 8–9, 20. Subsequent references are to this edition, apparently the only one, and are cited in the text.

25. Sidgwick, *The Grasshoppers* (London: Adam and Charles Black, 1895), pp. 37–38. This is apparently the only edition. In eighteen of the thirty-two Anglo-Jewish novels, the treatment of intermarriage, with or without conversion, undergoes a change in the nineteenth century from receiving uniform disapproval before 1887 to being treated as an accepted fact before the novel opens. After 1887 Anglo-Jewish novelists treat intermarriage from varied positions, with varying degrees of emphasis, and some, like Sidgwick, approve.

26. Picciotto, pp. 198–201, 364–66.

27. It is my contention that the stereotype of the domineering Jewish woman has its origin in the ghetto, where the wife frequently managed the home and business affairs. Although a husband was required by Jewish law to support his wife and family, he was equally aware that the greatest attainment for a Jew was to be a learned man. He therefore often ignored the problem of his family's support to study Jewish law, sometimes leaving his family for months to sit at the feet of a renowned rabbi. In this situation a wife without a wealthy father was faced with her family's support; she marketed the produce she grew, for example, and became a competent provider. It was but a short step from running her home and business to running her husband when he was at home.

28. Isidore G. Ascher, *The Doom of Destiny* (London: Diprose and Bateman, 1895), p. 30. Subsequent references are to this edition, apparently the only Amerian edition, and are cited in the text.

29. Samuel Gordon, *The Queen's Quandary* (London: Sands, 1903), p.

134. Subsequent references are to this edition, apparently the only one, and are cited in the text.

30. Gordon, *The Ferry of Fate* (New York: Duffield, 1907), p. 42. Subsequent references are to this edition, apparently the only American edition, and are cited in the text.

31. Gordon, *Unto Each Man His Own* (London: William Heinemann, 1904), pp. 65, 196. Subsequent references are to this edition, apparently the only one, and are cited in the text.

32. Charles Russell and H. Lewis, *The Jews in London: A Study of Racial Character and Present-Day Conditions (Being Two Essays Prepared for the Toynbee Trustees)* (New York: Thomas Y. Crowell, 1901), p. 89.

33. Samuel Gordon, *Sons of the Covenant; A Tale of London Jewry* (Philadelphia: The Jewish Publication Society of America, 1900), p. 323. Subsequent references are to this edition, apparently the only American edition, and are cited in the text.

34. Anthony Trollope, *Nina Balatka* (London: Oxford University Press, 1946), Chapter 6.

Chapter Three

1. Edward Bickersteth, *Christian Psalmody: A Collection of Above 700 Psalms, Hymns and Spiritual Songs* (London: L. B. Seeley and Sons, 1833), Hymn 405, as quoted by Tamke, p. 134.

2. Madame Brendlah, *Tales of A Jewess; Illustrating the Domestic Manners and Customs of the Jews; Interspersed with Original Anecdotes of Napoleon* (London: Simpkin, Marshall, 1838). Another apostate, Michael Solomon Alexander (1799−1845), converted in 1825 and became the first Anglican bishop of Jerusalem. His lectures include *The Hope of Israel* (1831). Because it and his other books are unobtainable, Alexander's attitude toward Judaism after he converted is regrettably unknown.

3. "Mr. D'Israeli's *Tancred*," *Edinburgh Review*, Am. Ed. 86 (July 1847): 73− 82.

4. Lucien Wolf, *Essays in Jewish History*, ed. Cecil Roth (London: Jewish Historical Society of England, 1934), p. 243; Joseph Jacobs and Lucien Wolf, eds. and comps., *Bibliotheca Anglo-Judaica: A Bibliographical Guide to Anglo-Jewish History* (London: Publication of the Anglo-Jewish Historical Exhibition, 3, 1888), identify Montefiore as Mrs. Horatio Montefiore and place her in the category of political and social writers on the basis of *A Few Words to the Jews, by One of Themselves* (1851). Calisch, who does not divide Anglo-Jewish authors by category, lists as publications for Charlotte Montefiore *The Way to Get Rich* (n.d.), *The Birthday* (n.d.), *Caleb Asher* (n.d.), and *A Few Words to the Jews* (1851). Of her works only *Caleb Asher* was located.

5. Charlotte Montefiore, *Caleb Asher* (Philadelphia: Jewish Publication Society, 1845), p. 93. Subsequent references are cited in the text.

6. Alois Brandl und Max Forster, *Jahrbuch der Deutschen Shakespeare-Gesellschaft* (Berlin-Schöneberg: Langenscheidtsche Verlagsbuchhandlung, 1911), p. 333; Alois Brandl und Heinrich Morf, *Archiv für das Studium der Neueren Sprachen und Literaturen* (Braunschweig: George Westermann, 1910), p. 216; Cecil Roth, *Magna Bibliotheca Anglo-Judaica: A Bibliographical Guide to Anglo-Jewish History* (London: Jewish Historical Society of England, 1937), pp. 74, 77.

Nathan Meritor, pseud. [Matthias Levy], *The Hasty Marriage; A Sketch of Modern Jewish Life* (London: Mann Nephews, 1857). Subsequent references are cited in the text.

7. Cecil Roth, *Magna Bibliotheca*, p. 63; *Encyclopedia Judaica*, XIV, cols. 1579–80.

8. Oswald John Simon, *The World and the Cloister*, 2 vols. (London: Chapman and Hall, 1890), I, 268–69.

9. Benjamin Farjeon, *Aaron the Jew* (London: Hutchinson, 1894), p. 322. Subsequent references are to this edition, the earliest English edition, and are cited in the text.

Chapter Four

1. For a detailed study of Jewish stereotypes in English literature see Modder, *The Jew;* Edgar Rosenberg, *From Shylock to Svengali: Jewish Stereotypes in English Fiction* (Stanford: Stanford University Press, 1960); Harold Fisch, *The Dual Image: A Study of the Figure of the Jew in English Literature* (London: Lincolns-Prager, 1959); Calisch, *The Jew;* Rabbi David Phillipson, *The Jew in English Fiction* (Cincinnati: Clarke, 1889); and Estelle Chevelier, "Characterization of the Jew in the Victorian Novel, 1864–1876," M.A. Thesis Emory University 1962. For a cogent discussion of the problem of stereotypical characterization, see Floyd Watkins, *The Death of Art* (Athens, Ga.: University of Georgia Press, 1970). Dates of English novels are from the *British Museum General Catalogue of Printed Books* and the *National Union Catalog Pre-1956 Imprints*.

2. See the London *Times*, 2, 9, 10, 13, 14 July 1830.

3. Eleanor Farjeon, *A Nursery in the Nineties* (London: Oxford University Press, 1960), pp. 26–37, 45–54. Subsequent references are cited in the text. *Encyclopedia Judaica*, VI, cols. 1185–86.

4. Tom Hood, *The Lost Link*, 3 vols. (London: Tinsley, 1868), II, 50–51.

5. Benjamin Farjeon, *At the Sign of the Silver Flagon* (New York: Harper and Bros., 1875), p. 63. Subsequent references are to this edition, the only American edition, and are cited in the text.

6. Farjeon, *Solomon Isaacs; A Novel* (Chicago: Donnelly, Loyd, 1877), p. 905. Subsequent references are to this edition and are cited in the text.

7. Farjeon, *Pride of Race* (Philadelphia: George W. Jacobs, 1901), pp. 100–101; see also p. 121. Subsequent references are to this edition and are cited in the text.

8. William Thackeray, "Codlingsby" (Centenary Editon, London: Macmillan, 1911), III, 159.

9. Anthony Trollope, *The Way We Live Now* (London: Oxford University Press, 1941), Chapter 4. Subsequent references are cited in the text.

Chapter Five

1. Emily Marian Harris, *Estelle* (London: George Bell, 1878).

2. Harris, *Benedictus* (London: George Bell, 1887).

3. For biographical information on Amy Levy, I am indebted to Beth-Zion Abrahams, "Amy Levy: Poet and Writer," *Anglo-Jewish Association Quarterly* VI: 3 (1960): 11–17, and to conversations with Mrs. Abrahams during August 1970.

4. Amy Levy, "Cohen of Trinity," *Gentlemen's Magazine* 166 (January–June 1889): 420.

5. As quoted by Abrahams, "Levy," pp. 12–13. Subsequent references to this article are cited in the text.

6. Amy Levy, *Reuben Sachs; A Sketch* (London: Macmillan, 1888), p. 25. Subsequent references are to this edition and are cited in the text.

7. *Encyclopedia Judaica*, VII, col. 77; *Dictionnaire Biographique Du Mouvement Ouvrier Francais* (Paris: Les Editions Ouvriers, 1975), XIII, 167; conversations with Mrs. Abrahams during August 1970. Less frequently, the year of Frankau's birth is cited as 1864.

8. Rebecca Schneider, *Bibliography of Jewish Life*, p. 16.

9. Frank Danby, pseud. [Julia Frankau], *Dr. Phillips; A Maida Vale Idyll*, 2nd ed. (London: Vizetelly, 1887), Preface. Subsequent references are to this edition and are cited in the text.

Chapter Six

1. Calisch, *The Jew*, p. 256; Conversation with Harold Mortlake, 7 August 1970.

2. George Watson, ed., *The New Cambridge Bibliography of English Literature,* III (Cambridge, England: University of Cambridge Press, 1969), col. 958.

3. Samuel Phillips, "Caleb Stukely," *Blackwood's Edinburgh Magazine* 51 (1842): 224–41, 306–22, 445–73, 585–608; 52 (1842): 35–60, 235–61, 374–78, 505–29, 614–40; 53 (1843): 33–61, 213–24, 314–37, 496–517, 651–73. Subsequent references are to this edition and are cited in the text by volume and page number.

4. Frank Danby, pseud. [Julia Frankau], *A Babe in Bohemia* (London: S. Blackett, 1889). This quote is from p. 94 of the third English edition, published in 1912 by Stanley Paul.

5. Frankau, *Pigs in Clover* (Philadelphia: J. B. Lippincott, 1903), p. 60. Subsequent references are to this edition, the first American edition, and are cited in the text.

6. Frankau, *The Sphinx's Lawyer* (New York: Frederick A. Stokes, 1906), p. 202. Subsequent references are to this edition, apparently the only American edition, and are cited in the text.

7. Harold Fisch, "Israel Zangwill," *Encyclopedia Judaica*, XVI, cols. 903 – 32; Annamarie Peterson, "Israel Zangwill (1864–1926): A Selected Bibliography," *Bulletin of Bibliography* (1969): 26:6 136–40. For full-length studies of Zangwill see Joseph Leftwich, *Israel Zangwill* (London: Clarke, 1957); Maurice Wohlgelernter, *Israel Zangwill: A Study* (New York: Columbia University Press, 1964); and Elsie Bonita Adams, *Israel Zangwill* (New York: Twayne, 1971).

8. Israel Zangwill, *Ghetto Tragedies* (New York: Macmillan, 1907, p. 74. Subsequent references are to this edition and are cited in the text.

9. Zangwill, *Ghetto Comedies* (New York: Macmillan, 1907), p. 195.

10. Zangwill, *The King of Schnorrers* (New York: Macmillan, 1894), p. 69. Subsequent references are to this edition and are cited in the text.

Chapter Seven

1. Charles Dickens, *Oliver Twist*, 4th ed. (1867; rpt. Baltimore: Penguin Books, 1966). George Du Maurier, *Trilby* (New York: Harper and Brothers, 1894). Subsequent references to both novels are to these editions and are cited in the text.

2. J. Hillis Miller, *Charles Dickens: The World of His Novels* (Cambridge, Mass.: Harvard University Press, 1965), pp. 47–50, 58–59, notes that Fagin lives in a dungeon which is his planning center of nefarious activities for the gang.

3. A Mrs. Eliza Davis began the controversy over Dickens's alleged anti-Semitism when she raised to the novelist the unfairness to Jews of the portrayal of Fagin. Edgar Johnson, *Charles Dickens: His Tragedy and Triumph* (New York: Simon and Schuster, 1952), I, 1010–12, reports that to Mrs. Davis Dickens justified Fagin as being Jewish "because it unfortunately was true of the time to which the story refers, that that class of criminal almost invariably was a Jew." Dickens added, "I make mention of Fagin as a Jew because he is one of the Jewish people and because it conveys that kind of idea of him, which I would give my readers of a Chinaman by calling him a Chinese. . . . I have no feeling towards the Jewish people but a friendly one. I always speak well of them, whether in public or in private, and bear testimony (as I ought to do) to their perfect good faith in such transactions as I have ever had with them. And in my *Child's History of England*, I have lost no opportunity of setting forth their cruel persecution in old times." Modern discussions of Fagin's Jewishness include Edgar Johnson, "Dickens, Fagin and Mr. Riah," *Commentary* 9 (1950): 47–50; Lauriat Lane, Jr., "Dickens' Archetypal Jew," *PMLA* 73 (March 1958): 95–101; and Harry Stone, "Dickens and the Jews," *Victorian Studies* 11 (March 1959): 223–53.

Selected Bibliography

PRIMARY SOURCES

1. Anglo-Jewish Novelists' Works about Jews (asterisk indicates short stories; first date of publication in England is cited except where it was unobtainable).

ABRAHAM, PHILLIP. *Autobiography of a Jewish Gentleman*. London, 1860. Not located.

AGUILAR, GRACE. *Israel Defended* by Orobio de Castro, translated from the unpublished French version. London: J. Wertheimer, 1838.

————. *The Spirit of Judaism*, ed. Isaac Leeser. Philadelphia: C. Sherman, 1842.

————. *Records of Israel** (two tales later incorporated in *Home Scenes and Heart Studies*). London: J. Mortimer, 1844.

————. *Women of Israel*. London: R. Groomridge, 1845.

————. *The Jewish Faith, Its Spiritual Consolation, Moral Guidance, and Immortal Hope*. London: R. Groombridge, 1846.

————. "History of the Jews in England." *Chambers' Miscellany*, 1847.

————. *The·Vale of Cedars; or, the Martyr*. London: R. Groombridge, 1850.

————. *Home Scenes and Heart Studies.** London: R. Groombridge, 1853.

————. *Sabbath Thoughts and Sacred Communings*. London: R. Groombridge, 1853.

————. *Collected Works*. 8 vols. London: R. Groombridge, 1861.

ASCHER, ISIDORE G. *The Doom of Destiny*. London: Diprose, 1895.

FARJEON, BENJAMIN L. *At the Sign of the Silver Flagon*. 3 vols. London: Tinsley, 1876.

————. *Solomon Isaacs; A Novel*. London: Tinsley, 1877.

————. *Aaron the Jew*. London: Hutchinson, 1894.

————. *Pride of Race*. London: Hutchinson, 1900.

FRANKAU, JULIA. [Frank Danby, pseud.] *Dr. Phillips; A Maida Vale Idyll*. London: Vizetelly, 1887.

————. *A Babe in Bohemia*. London: S. Blackett, 1889.

————. *Pigs in Clover*. London: Heinemann, 1903.

————. *The Sphinx's Lawyer*. London: Heinemann, 1906.

GORDON, SAMUEL. *A Handful of Exotics; Scenes and Incidents Chiefly of Russo-Jewish Life.** London: Methuen, 1897.

————. *The Daughters of Shem.** London: Greenberg, 1898.

————. *Sons of the Covenant; A Tale of London Jewry*. London: Sands, 1900.

_____ . *Strangers at the Gate; Tales of Russian Jewry.** Philadelphia: Jewish Publication Society of America, 1902.

_____ . *The Queen's Quandary; A Romance.* London: Sands, 1903.

_____ . *Unto Each Man His Own.* London: Heinemann, 1904.

_____ . *The Ferry of Fate.* London: Chatto, 1906.

_____ . *God's Remnants.** London: J. M. Dent, 1916.

HARRIS, EMILY MARIAN. *Estelle.* 2 vols. London: George Bell, 1878.

_____ . *Benedictus.* 2 vols. London: Geoge Bell, 1887.

LEOPOLD, DAVID L. *A Peal of Merry Bells.** London, 1880. Not located.

LEVETUS, CELIA MOSS. *The King's Physician and Other Tales.** Birmingham, England: Hinton, 1865.

LEVY, AMY. *Reuben Sachs; A Sketch.* London: Macmillan, 1888.

_____ . "Cohen of Trinity." *Gentlemen's Magazine* 266 (May 1889): 417—24.

LEVY, MATTHIAS. [Nathan Meritor, pseud.] *The Hasty Marriage; A Sketch of Modern Jewish Life.* London: Mann Nephews, 1857.

MONTEFIORE, CHARLOTTE. *Caleb Asher.* Philadelphia: Jewish Publication Society, 1845.

_____ . *A Few Words to the Jews, by One of Themselves.* London, 1851. Not located.

_____ . *The Way to Get Rich.* Not located.

_____ . *The Birthday.* Not located.

MOSS, CELIA and MARIAN. *The Romance of Jewish History.** 3 vols. London: Saunders and Otley, 1840.

_____ . *Tales of Jewish History.** 3 vols. London: Miller and Field, 1843.

PHILLIPS, SAMUEL. "Caleb Stukely." *Blackwood's Edinburgh Magazine* 51, 52, 53 (1842—1843).

_____ . "Moses and Son." *Blackwood's Edinburgh Magazine* 59 (March 1846): 294—305.

SIDGWICK, MRS. ALFRED. [Mrs. Andrew Dean, pseud.] *Lesser's Daughter.* London: Unwin, 1894.

_____ . *Isaac Eller's Money.* London: Unwin, 1889.

_____ . *The Grasshoppers.* London: Adam and Charles Black, 1895.

_____ . *A Woman with a Future.* London: Adam and Charles Black, 1896.

_____ . *Scenes from Jewish Life.** London: Edward Arnold, 1904.

_____ . *Home Life in Germany.* London: Methuen, 1908.

_____ . *The Devil's Cradle.* New York: W. J. Watt, 1918.

_____ . *Iron Cousins.* New York: W. J. Watt, 1919.

_____ . *Refugee.* London: Collins, 1934.

SIMON, OSWALD JOHN. *The World and the Cloister.* 2 vols. London: Chapman and Hall, 1890.

STONE, I. *A Historical Sketch of a London Tailor.* London, 1885. Not located.

ZANGWILL, ISRAEL. *Children of the Ghetto; A Study of a Peculiar People.* London: Heinemann, 1892.

_____ . *Ghetto Tragedies.** London: McClure and Co., 1893.

———. *The King of Schnorrers*. London: Heinemann, 1894.

———. *Dreamers of the Ghetto*.* London: Heinemann, 1898.

———. *Ghetto Comedies*.* London: Heinemann, 1907.

———. *The Voice of Jerusalem*. London: Heinemann, 1920.

———. *The Works of Israel Zangwill*. 14 vols. London: Globe, 1925.

2. Some Conversionist Novels

BRENDLAH, MADAM. *Tales of a Jewess; Illustrating the Domestic Customs and Manners of the Jews; Interspersed with Original Anecdotes of Napoleon.* London: Simpkin and Marshall, 1838.

BRISTOW, AMELIA. *Emma de Lissau; A Narrative of Striking Vicissitudes and Peculiar Trials; with Explanatory Notes, Illustrative of the Manners and Customs of the Jews.* 2 vols. London: T. Gardiner, 1828.

———. *The Orphans of Lissau, and Other Interesting Narratives, Immediately Connected with Jewish Customs, Domestic and Religious; with Explanatory Notes.* 2 vols. London: T. Gardiner, 1830.

———. *Sophia De Lissau; A Portraiture of the Jews, of the Nineteenth Century; Being an Outline of Their Religious and Domestic Habits; with Explanatory Notes.* 4th ed. London: T. Gardiner, 1833.

———. *Rosette and Miriam; or, the Twin Sisters; A Jewish Narrative of the Eighteenth Century.* London: Charles Tilt, 1837.

STERN, CHARLOTTE ELIZABETH. *Eliezer; or, Suffering for Christ.* London: Partridge, 1877.

WASSERMANN, LILIAS. [Adam Lilburn, pseud.] *A Tragedy in Marble.* London: Chatto and Windus, 1898.

WHEELER, ELIZABETH. *From Petticoat Lane to Rotten Row; or, the Child of the Ghetto.* London: John Heywood, 1900.

SECONDARY SOURCES

ABRAHAMS, BETH-ZION. "Amy Levy: Poet and Writer." *Anglo-Jewish Association Quarterly* I: 3 (1960): 11–17. In this excellent discussion of Levy's ideas and work, Abrahams charts the breadth of Levy's Jewish interests.

———. "Grace Aguilar: A Centenary Tribute." *Transactions of the Jewish Historical Society of England* 16 (1952): 137–48. A capable survey which placed Aguilar's Jewish ideas and works in the context of Anglo-Judaism.

ARIS, STEPHEN. *But There Are No Jews in England.* New York: Stein and Day, 1970. Aris examines the impact of Jews on English business history since 1656, stressing Anglo-Jews' desire to remain inconspicuous as Jews and to be considered genuine Englishmen.

BALDWIN, EDWARD CHAUNCEY "The Jewish Genius in Literature, A Study of Three Modern Men of Letters." *Menorah Journal* I: 3 (June 1915): 164–

72. Baldwin briefly reviews the works of Heine, Disraeli, and Zangwill. He finds Zangwill inconsistent on the basis of his short stories and a play, but a writer "in whom the ancient ideals of Israel live again."

CALISCH, EDWARD N. *The Jew in English Literature as Author and as Subject.* Richmond, Virginia: Bell, 1909. Informative early analysis of the ways Jews were historically portrayed in literature and the types of literature written by Anglo-Jews. The broadest and most helpful bibliography of Anglo-Jewish writers. Calisch divides his bibliography into non-Jewish and Jewish authors but does not consistently list dates of publication.

CHEVELIER, ESTELLE. *Characterization of the Jew in the Victorian Novel, 1864–1876.* M.A. Thesis, Emory University 1962. Discussion of the figure of the Jew is divided into positive and negative stereotypes and the humanized Jew, created by George Eliot.

COLBY, ROBERT. *Fiction with a Purpose: Major and Minor Nineteenth-Century Novels.* Bloomington: Indiana University Press, 1967. Valuable for the reader whose interest is propaganda fiction.

FARJEON, ELEANOR. *A Nursery in the Nineties.* London: Oxford University Press, 1960. A rambling, often disjointed but informative book about Benjamin Farjeon, his parents, his wife, and his children.

FISCH, HAROLD. *The Dual Image.* London: Lincolns-Prager, 1959. Fisch perceptively studies the idealized and the negative stereotypes of the Jew in English literature.

FREEDMAN, MAURICE, ed. *A Minority in Britain: Social Studies of the Anglo-Jewish Community.* London: Vallentine, Mitchell, 1955. Examines Jewish social institutions to view the impact of assimilation on the Jewish community and its leaders.

GAER, JOSEPH. *The Legend of the Wandering Jew.* New York: Mentor, 1961.

GARTNER, LLOYD P. *The Jewish Immigrant in England, 1870–1914.* London: George Allen and Unwin, 1960. A careful examination of the immigrant and his community, detailing his religious practices, the trades he entered, and his economic and social impact.

GEORGE, M. DOROTHY. *London Life in the Eighteenth Century.* New York: Knopf, 1925. Jewish gangs and their impact on English life are briefly discussed.

GERSONI, LEON. "A Summary of English Jewish Fiction." *Maccabean* 20 (1911): 171–73. Reviews primarily twentieth-century Anglo-Jewish novelists, noting that Zangwill and Gordon portray ghetto life accurately, but concludes that with the passing of interest in the ghetto Anglo-Jewish fiction has not yet been created.

GOULD, KENNETH M. *They Got the Blame: The Story of Scapegoats in History.* New York: Association Press, 1942.

HAY, MALCOLM. *Europe and the Jews: The Pressures of Christendom on the People of Israel for 1900 Years.* Boston: Beacon Press, 1960. An apologist study, valuable for its non-Jewish view of anti-Semitism.

HENKIN, LEO J. "Problem and Digressions in the Victorian Novel, 1860–

1900." *Bulletin of Bibliography* 18: 5 (September-December 1944): 105 – 107. Lists novels mainly by non-Jews.

HYAMSON, ALBERT M. "Bibliography of Books and Articles of Jewish Interest that have appeared in British and American Periodicals from Nov. 1, 1903 to May 15, 1904." *Jewish Literary Annual* 1 (1903): 109 – 11.

————. *A History of the Jews in England*. 2nd ed. London: Metheun, 1928. Until Roth's, the standard history.

————. *The Sephardim of England: A History of the Spanish and Portuguese Jewish Community, 1492 – 1951*. London: Methuen, 1951. Detailed account of Sephardic religious, economic, and social life in England.

JACOBS, JOSEPH. *Studies in Jewish Statistics, Social, Vital and Anthropometric*. London: D. Nutt, 1891. Jacobs provides figures on the origins, occupations, economic positions, and professions of Jews in England during the eighties.

————, and WOLF, LUCIEN, eds. and comps. *Bibliotheca Anglo-Judaica: A Bibliographical Guide to Anglo-Jewish History*. London: Publication of the Anglo-Jewish Historical Exhibition, 3, 1888.

JOHNSON, EDGAR. "Dickens, Fagin and Mr. Riah." *Commentary* 9 (1950): 47 – 50. Dickens's biographer claims that, aside from the designation "the Jew," Fagin has none of the usual physical or religious attributes written into a Jewish character.

LANDA, M[EYER] J[ACK]. *The Jew in Drama*. New York: William Morrow, 1927. Landa follows the characterization of the Jew in English drama from the morality plays forward.

LANE, LAURIAT, JR. "Dickens' Archetypal Jew." *PMLA* 73 (March 1958): 95 – 101.

LEBOWICH, JOSEPH. "Contemporary Anglo-Jewish Writers." *American Hebrew* 75 (1904): 632 – 34. Lists and very briefly reviews the kinds of writing turn-of-the-century Anglo-Jews were publishing.

LIPMAN, V[IVIAN] D[AVID]. *Social History of the Jews in England: 1850 – 1950*. London: Watts, 1954. A fascinating and detailed study together with his *Three Centuries* and Roth's *History of the Jews*, this is mandatory reading for anyone interested in Anglo-Jewry.

————, ed. *Three Centuries of Anglo-Jewish History*. Cambridge, England: Jewish Historical Society of England, 1961. Informative, factual essays.

LUKÁCS, GEORG. *The Historical Novel*. London: Merlin Press, 1962.

MAISON, MARGARET M. *The Victorian Vision: Studies in the Religious Novel*. New York: Sheed and Ward, 1961. Christian religious groups are examined through the fiction each produced.

MAYHEW, HENRY. *London Labour and the London Poor*. 4 vols., 1861 – 1862; rpt. New York: Dover, 1968. In this exhaustive, firsthand account, poor Jews and their occupations and attitudes as well as the attitudes of other poor people about Jews are presented especially in the first two volumes. Jewish assistance to the needy is documented.

MITCHELL, B. R., and DEANE, PHYLLIS. *Abstract of British Historical Statistics.* Cambridge, England: Cambridge University Press, 1962.

MODDER, MONTAGU FRANK. *The Jew in the Literature of England.* 1939; rpt. New York: Meridian Books, 1960. Pairs chapters on the Jew in politics and in literature. Modder is sometimes misinformed on Anglo-Jewish fiction. Bibliography broad but incomplete on Anglo-Jewish authors.

PHILLIPSON, DAVID. *The Jew in English Fiction.* Cincinnati: Clarke, 1889. An early and absorbing discussion of Jewish characters depicted by English authors, written to answer the question of whether the introduction of a character who is Jewish is legitimate.

PICCIOTTO, JAMES. *Sketches of Anglo-Jewish History.* London: Trubner, 1875. Written primarily for a Jewish audience, this is one of the earliest Victorian examinations of Anglo-Jewry.

ROSENBERG, EDGAR. *From Shylock to Svengali: Jewish Stereotypes in English Fiction.* Stanford, Calif.: Stanford University Press, 1960. Rosenberg divides his densely packed and valuable study into the major stereotypes and chronologically analyzes major and minor characters.

ROTH, CECIL. *A History of the Jews in England.* London: Oxford University Press, 1941. The standard history by one of the outstanding twentieth-century scholars of Judaica. Roth brings broad and deep knowledge to bear on Anglo-Jewish history, as on other allied subjects, making his work fascinating reading.

———. *A History of the Marranos.* Philadelphia: Jewish Publication Society of America, 1947. The standard history, well-written and scholarly, valuable for historical data as well as cultural information.

———, ed. *Magna Bibliotheca Anglo-Judaica: A Bibliographical Guide to Anglo-Jewish History.* London: The Jewish Historical Society of England, 1937.

———. "The Jew in the Literature of England.." *Menorah Journal* 28:1 (1940): 122–25. Roth finds Modder's book adds much information previously unknown about the nineteenth century but is deficient, notably about the eighteenth and early nineteenth centuries, and thus is not the "definitive study."

———. "Wellsprings of European Literature." *Menorah Journal* 25:3 (1937): 340–49. Demonstrates Jewish contributions to European civilization and literature.

RUSSELL, C., and LEWIS, H. S. *The Jew in London: A Study of Racial Character and Present-Day Conditions (Being Two Essays Prepared for the Toynbee Trustees).* New York: Thomas Y. Crowell, 1901. Two essays on the immigrant, one from the Christian and one from the Jewish viewpoint. The former, which reads like propaganda for restriction of immigration, argues from the disparaging position that English Jews and English Christians have more in common than do English Jews and foreign Jews.

SALOMON, SIDNEY. *The Jews of Britain*. London: Jerrolds, 1938.

SCHNEIDER, REBECCA. *Bibliography of Jewish Life in the Fiction of America and England*. Albany: New York State Library School, 1916. Divided by countries with which the works deal.

STONE, HARRY. "Dickens and the Jews," *Victorian Studies* 11 (March 1959): 223−53. Stone avers that Dickens's revisions subsequent to the 1838 edition, which greatly eliminated the term "the Jew" in the latter third of the novel, also eliminated Fagin's main link with the Jews.

TAMKE, SUSAN S. *Make a Joyful Noise unto the Lord: Hymns as a Reflection of Victorian Social Attitudes*. Athens, Ohio: University of Ohio Press, 1978. Especially good discussion of the hymns of missions to the Jews.

TRACHTENBERG, JOSHUA. *The Devil and the Jews: The Medieval Conception of the Jew and Its Relation to Modern Anti-Semitism*. New Haven: Yale University Press, 1943. Scholarly, absorbing study.

WEINBERGER, PHILIP M. "The Social and Religious Thought of Grace Aguilar (1816−1847)." Diss. New York University 1970.

Index

DEC 6 '71	Dec 6 '71		
12.			
DEC 13 71			
GAYLORD			PRINTED IN U.S A.